Salamanca

Travel Guide 2025

Top Attractions, Hidden Gems, and Local Insights for an
Unforgettable Spanish Experience

By

Joe Morgan

TABLE OF CONTENTS

Chapter 1: Introduction to Salamanca

Brief Overview of Salamanca

Nestled in the heart of Spain, Salamanca is a city that exudes a captivating blend of history, culture, and academic prestige. Located in the region of Castile and León, it is renowned for its striking architectural heritage, vibrant student life, and deep cultural roots. Although relatively small in terms of population, with just over 150,000 residents, Salamanca holds a significant place in both Spanish and global history, making it a prime destination for travelers from all over the world.

Salamanca is often referred to as the "Golden City" due to the warm, golden hue of its sandstone buildings that glow beautifully under the sun. The city's charm is further enhanced by its winding streets, impressive cathedrals, quaint squares, and bustling markets, offering visitors a chance to step back in time while still enjoying modern amenities.

The city's beauty is not limited to its architecture. Salamanca is home to the world-renowned University of Salamanca, one of the oldest universities in Europe, which has been the intellectual center of the region for centuries. This university has attracted scholars, students, and academics from all corners of the globe, making the city a hub of knowledge and a symbol of Spain's commitment to education and learning.

Salamanca is more than just a beautiful city; it is a place steeped in history and tradition. Its streets echo with the footsteps of Spanish royalty, philosophers, artists, and intellectuals. The city has also been a witness to pivotal moments in Spanish history, including the Spanish Civil War and the Inquisition, which have shaped not only the city but the nation as a whole.

For visitors in 2025, Salamanca offers an immersive journey into Spain's past, a window into its rich cultural tapestry, and an invitation to explore its vibrant present. Whether you're wandering through its medieval streets, admiring its impressive monuments, or sitting in one of its lively cafés, Salamanca promises to leave you with lasting memories.

Historical Significance

Salamanca's history is as rich and diverse as its architecture. The city's roots trace back to the Roman era, with evidence of Roman settlements still visible today, including the remains of bridges and other structures that highlight the early foundations of Salamanca's significance. The city's strategic location along the Tormes River allowed it to thrive as a key settlement during the Roman Empire, and its prominence grew as the centuries passed.

By the 8th century, the city had fallen under the rule of the Moors, and it was during this period that Salamanca experienced considerable cultural and architectural growth. The influence of Moorish Spain is still visible in some of the city's more intricate architectural details, blending Roman and Islamic styles that were a hallmark of the era.

However, it is the University of Salamanca that truly shaped the city's historical significance. Founded in 1218 by King Alfonso IX, the university quickly became a center of learning and scholarship, attracting students and intellectuals from all over Europe and beyond. It was here that the famous Spanish scholar and writer, Fray Luis de León, taught, and where the renowned philosopher Miguel de Unamuno served as rector in the early 20th century. The university's influence on Spanish culture, language, and thought cannot be overstated, and it continues to play a key role in Salamanca's identity to this day.

Throughout its history, Salamanca has witnessed several key events that have shaped Spain's political and cultural landscape. During the Spanish Inquisition in the late 15th and early 16th centuries, the city became one of the primary centers for religious trials. The city's Cathedral, with its elaborate architecture and spiritual importance, was at the heart of the religious movements that swept through Spain.

Salamanca was also a key city during the Spanish Civil War. Though not a battleground, the city was a hub for political activity and intellectual debate, with many scholars using their voices to either support or oppose the war. This period of history left a deep mark on the city, with certain buildings and sites still bearing the scars of the conflict.

In the 20th century, Salamanca's university continued to be a center of thought and innovation, and it played a significant role in Spain's transition to democracy following the death of Franco. The city's educational institutions, rich in history, fostered a new generation of thinkers and leaders who helped guide Spain into the modern era.

Today, Salamanca remains a city of deep historical significance, offering visitors the chance to walk through centuries of Spanish history, from the Roman era to the modern day. The historical monuments, museums, and landmarks that dot the city serve as reminders of the many chapters that have shaped this iconic Spanish city.

Why Visit Salamanca in 2025?

Salamanca is an ideal destination for 2025, offering a dynamic blend of history, culture, and modern life that appeals to a wide range of travelers. Whether you're a history enthusiast, a lover of architecture, or someone simply looking for a charming Spanish city to explore, Salamanca provides an unforgettable experience. Here's why 2025 is the perfect time to visit this timeless city:

1. Rich Cultural Heritage

Salamanca is a city where history and culture come alive. The city is home to some of Spain's most impressive landmarks, including the Old and New Cathedrals, the University of Salamanca, and the Plaza Mayor. Visitors can wander through narrow medieval streets, explore hidden courtyards, and admire centuries-old buildings that tell the stories of Salamanca's past. For those interested in Spanish history, the city offers an unparalleled chance to experience the cultural richness that shaped the nation.

2. Vibrant Student Life

With its world-renowned university, Salamanca is one of Spain's most important student cities. In 2025, the city will continue to be home to thousands of international students, creating a lively and youthful atmosphere that infuses the city with energy. Visitors can enjoy the vibrant café culture, attend events and festivals, or simply stroll through the university's historic campus, where the legacy of intellectuals continues to thrive.

3. Dynamic Arts and Events Scene

Salamanca is home to a flourishing arts and culture scene, with numerous galleries, museums, and performance spaces showcasing local and international talent. In 2025, the city will host a variety of cultural events, including music festivals, theater performances, and art exhibitions, providing visitors with plenty of opportunities to experience the best of Salamanca's artistic offerings. The city's calendar of festivals is filled with exciting events such as the Fiesta de la Virgen de la Vega, a celebration of local traditions, and the International Film Festival, which draws filmmakers and cinephiles from around the world.

4. Culinary Delights

Salamanca offers a fantastic array of food experiences, from traditional Spanish dishes to contemporary culinary creations. Visitors in 2025 will be able to enjoy delicious local specialties like *jamón ibérico* (Iberian ham), *cochinillo* (suckling pig), and *tapas* at the city's many restaurants and bars. The Plaza Mayor, with its bustling cafés and vibrant atmosphere, is a perfect spot for enjoying a coffee or a traditional Spanish meal while watching the world go by.

For those who enjoy wine, Salamanca is well-positioned in the Castilla y León wine region, offering access to some of Spain's best wines. In 2025, visitors can take wine tours, visit vineyards, and indulge in tastings that showcase the region's rich winemaking heritage.

5. A Place for Reflection and Relaxation

Beyond its historical and cultural offerings, Salamanca is a city of tranquility. With its peaceful parks, scenic riverside walks along the Tormes River, and charming plazas, it offers a relaxing environment for travelers seeking a break from the bustle of modern life. The city's relatively small size makes it easy to explore on foot, allowing visitors to immerse themselves in the city's beauty at a leisurely pace.

6. Accessibility and Modern Amenities

Salamanca is well-connected to other major Spanish cities, including Madrid, with regular train services and easy road access. In 2025, the city continues to provide modern amenities for visitors, including high-quality accommodation options, excellent public transport, and a range of services that cater to international tourists. The city also boasts a strong commitment to sustainability, making it a great choice for eco-conscious travelers.

7. A Growing Hub for International Tourism

In recent years, Salamanca has been increasingly recognized as a top travel destination. As the city continues to grow in popularity, 2025 promises to be an exciting year for tourism in Salamanca. The city's unique combination of historical charm, cultural vibrancy, and modern conveniences makes it an ideal destination for travelers seeking an authentic Spanish experience.

Salamanca in 2025 represents the perfect blend of old-world charm and modern vitality. Whether you're captivated by the history, enamored by the culture, or simply looking to enjoy a relaxed and beautiful city, Salamanca offers a unique and rewarding experience for every traveler. The city's long-standing academic tradition, its architectural splendor, and its vibrant student atmosphere make it a place worth visiting, ensuring that anyone who visits in 2025 will be immersed in the timeless allure of this remarkable Spanish city.

Chapter 2: Getting to Salamanca

Salamanca, one of Spain's most charming cities, is well-connected by air, rail, and bus, offering several ways for visitors to reach this historical destination. Whether you're flying into Spain or traveling by train from other cities, there are plenty of options to suit your preferences. This chapter breaks down the best ways to travel to Salamanca, offering you detailed information about airports, train stations, and public transportation once you arrive in the city.

Best Ways to Travel to Salamanca

1. By Air

Salamanca is served by Salamanca Airport (IATA: SLM), located about 14 kilometers east of the city center. Although the airport handles a limited number of international flights, it is primarily used for domestic flights within Spain, such as to and from Palma de Mallorca, Valencia, and Ibiza. It also serves as a base for seasonal charter flights, making it a convenient option for travelers during peak holiday seasons.

For international travelers, it is often more practical to fly into one of Spain's major international airports, such as Madrid-Barajas Adolfo Suárez Airport (MAD), which is approximately 200 kilometers away from Salamanca. From there, you can take a bus or train to Salamanca, or hire a car for the scenic drive through the Spanish countryside. While Salamanca's airport has limited facilities, including a small terminal and basic amenities like a café and restrooms, it remains an important entry point for those traveling to the city by air.

Traveling from Salamanca Airport to the City Center:

Upon arrival at Salamanca Airport, there are several ways to get to the city center. While there are no direct public buses from the airport to the city, taxis are available and provide a convenient option for travelers. A taxi ride typically takes about 20 minutes and costs between €20-€25, depending on traffic and the time of day. Alternatively, private transfer services can be arranged in advance for a smoother experience. Renting a car is also a viable option for those who wish to explore the surrounding areas during their stay.

2. By Train

Salamanca is connected to other Spanish cities via the Salamanca Train Station (Estación de Tren de Salamanca). The city's main railway station is located at Plaza de la Estación, just a few kilometers from the city center. While Salamanca is not part of Spain's high-speed AVE train network, the station is well connected to Madrid, Valladolid, and other major cities, making train travel a viable and convenient option.

The Madrid to Salamanca train route, operated by Renfe, typically takes about 3 to 3.5 hours, with frequent services available throughout the day. Trains are comfortable and offer a relaxing journey through the Spanish countryside. For travelers coming from Madrid, the Estación de Chamartín is the main train station to catch trains to Salamanca. Train services to Salamanca run regularly, especially during the daytime, and are well-equipped with amenities such as air-conditioning, comfortable seating, and food options.

Traveling from the Train Station to the City Center:
Once you arrive at the Salamanca Train Station, it's a short taxi ride to the city center. Taxis are available directly outside the station, and the fare to central Salamanca is typically around €8-€10. Alternatively, for those who prefer public transport, buses run from the station to various parts of the city, including the main tourist areas.

3. By Bus

Salamanca is also well-served by long-distance buses, with the Salamanca Bus Station (Estación de Autobuses de Salamanca) located in the southeastern part of the city, around 3 kilometers from the city center. The bus station offers services from several major cities in Spain, including Madrid, Valladolid, and Zaragoza, as well as regional routes within Castilla y León.

Buses from Madrid take approximately 2.5 to 3 hours, depending on the specific route and time of day. Bus services are operated by various companies, including ALSA, which is one of Spain's largest bus operators. In addition to long-distance buses, there are regional buses connecting Salamanca with nearby towns and villages, making it a convenient option for travelers arriving from smaller locations.

Traveling from the Bus Station to the City Center:
From the Salamanca Bus Station, taxis are available to take you into the city center. The ride typically costs between €8-€12, depending on the traffic and destination. Alternatively, there are local buses that connect the bus station to the main parts of the city, including the Plaza Mayor and the University of Salamanca. Travelers who enjoy walking can reach the city center on foot in about 30 minutes.

Airport and Train Information

Salamanca Airport (LESA)

Salamanca's airport is relatively small but sufficient for the city's needs. Here's what you need to know:

- **Location**: The airport is located around 14 kilometers from the city center.

- **Domestic and Seasonal Flights**: Mainly services domestic routes and a few international seasonal flights.

- **Facilities**: Limited amenities, including a small café, restrooms, and a waiting area.

- **Transportation to City Center**: Taxis are available for the 20-minute journey into the city. Alternatively, private transfer services can be arranged in advance, or car rental is an option for those wanting more flexibility.

Salamanca Train Station

The Estación de Tren de Salamanca is the primary railway station in the city. It offers:

- **Location**: The train station is located just a few kilometers from Salamanca's city center, making it convenient for travelers arriving by train.

- **Services**: Regular train services to Madrid, Valladolid, and other major Spanish cities. Trains are typically comfortable, with services including air-conditioning and food options.

- **Transportation to City Center**: Taxis are readily available at the station, providing an affordable and convenient way to reach the city center. There are also local buses for public transport options.

Public Transportation Tips

While Salamanca is a relatively small city, it is still well-equipped with public transportation to help visitors get around. The city's compact size means that many of the main attractions are within walking distance of each other, but for those who prefer using public transport, here are some tips.

1. Urban Buses

Salamanca has an extensive and efficient bus network operated by Salamanca de Transportes S.A.. The city's bus system is well-organized, and routes connect all major areas of the city, from the historic center to the university district, as well as more residential and outlying areas.

- **Tickets**: A single bus ride within the city typically costs about €1.05. Bus tickets can be purchased directly from the driver. For those planning to use the bus more frequently, there is a multi-ride pass that can offer discounts on fares.

- **Abono Transporte**: If you plan on using public transport frequently, consider purchasing the Abono Transporte card, which allows for discounted fares. The card costs around €2, with a minimum top-up of €5. It is a great option for visitors who want to explore the city extensively and use public transport regularly.

2. Taxis

Taxis are easily available throughout Salamanca, and the city's relatively small size means that getting a taxi is generally quick and convenient. Taxis can be hailed directly from the street or booked in advance.

- **Taxi Fares**: Taxi fares are reasonable, with a typical ride within the city costing between €5-€10, depending on the distance and time of day. The fare may increase if you are traveling during peak hours or on holidays, so it's always a good idea to confirm the price with the driver before starting your journey.

- **Taxi Booking**: While taxis are readily available, you can also book a taxi through various mobile apps or by calling a local taxi company. This is especially useful if you're traveling during busy periods or need a taxi at a specific time.

3. Car Rentals

For those who prefer more flexibility during their stay, renting a car is a great option. Several car rental agencies operate in Salamanca, with offices located at key spots such as the train station, bus station, and airport. Renting a car gives you the freedom to explore Salamanca and its surrounding regions at your own pace.

- **Requirements**: A valid driving license and a credit card are typically required. Rental companies may also have minimum age requirements, so check these details before booking. Car rental services in Salamanca are straightforward, and you'll find a range of vehicles to suit your needs, from compact cars to larger family vehicles.

- **Parking**: While Salamanca's city center is very pedestrian-friendly, there are designated parking zones for those who choose to drive. The city has several underground parking lots, and some areas provide free parking outside the main tourist zones. However, parking in central areas can be limited, so it's advisable to check the availability of parking in advance.

Chapter 3: Best Time to Visit Salamanca

Seasonal Guide

Salamanca, with its charming medieval streets, breathtaking architecture, and rich cultural atmosphere, offers a distinctive experience no matter when you visit. The city's climate, influenced by its inland location in the Castile and León region, creates noticeable seasonal changes that will shape your visit. Whether you seek warm weather and lively summer festivals, or a more tranquil and cool atmosphere during the off-season, Salamanca has something to offer in every season.

Spring (March to May)

Spring is one of the best times to visit Salamanca. The temperatures during this time are mild, making it a perfect season for outdoor exploration. March brings the first signs of warmth, with daytime temperatures reaching around 13°C (55°F), and nights cooling to about 3°C (37°F). As the city emerges from the colder winter months, you'll witness a gentle awakening as flowers bloom and the city's famous green spaces start to flourish. By

April, temperatures rise to around 16°C (61°F), and the days become noticeably longer, offering more daylight hours for sightseeing.

In May, temperatures typically reach the low 20s°C (70°F), providing a pleasant climate for walking tours through the city's historic streets, gardens, and parks. This is also a time when Salamanca's cultural calendar starts to come alive. The Semana Santa (Holy Week) celebrations in late March or early April are a major event, with elaborate processions, religious ceremonies, and cultural performances. If you're visiting Salamanca in May, you'll also have the chance to enjoy the Feria de Teatro (Theatre Fair), an event that brings together theatrical performances and street art that showcase both national and international talent.

Summer (June to August)

Summer in Salamanca can be quite hot, with temperatures frequently soaring above 30°C (86°F), especially in July and August. If you enjoy sunny weather and don't mind the heat, this is the time when Salamanca is most vibrant, with tourists and locals taking part in various outdoor activities. The long summer days offer plenty of opportunities to explore the city's architectural marvels, including the Plaza Mayor, the University of Salamanca, and the Cathedrals, all under the bright Spanish sun.

In addition to the warm weather, summer brings numerous cultural events, making it a lively time to experience Salamanca. The International Arts Festival in July is one of the most notable, attracting a wide variety of artists and performers, including musicians, dancers, and actors from around the world. This event fills the city with artistic energy, as performances take place in various venues, including theaters, outdoor spaces, and even the streets.

While Salamanca is bustling with visitors in the summer, it's important to note that prices for accommodation and attractions tend to be higher, and the crowds can be overwhelming, especially around popular tourist sites. Despite this, if you're looking for a festive and energetic atmosphere, summer is an excellent choice.

Autumn (September to November)

Autumn in Salamanca offers a more relaxed and temperate atmosphere, as the weather begins to cool down after the intense summer heat. September starts off warm with highs around 25°C (77°F), but temperatures gradually drop as the months progress. By November, daytime temperatures range from 10-15°C (50-59°F), and the crisp air creates a pleasant atmosphere for exploring the city's outdoor spaces and historical landmarks.

Autumn is also one of the best times for sightseeing without the summer crowds, as many tourists have returned home, and the city's attractions are less congested. The beautiful changing colors of the leaves in Salamanca's parks and along the Tormes River provide a stunning backdrop for walks. The Salamanca Fair, celebrated in early September, is a major event that features concerts, parades, and traditional festivities, offering a perfect chance to experience the city's culture in a lively setting.

Autumn is also the time when Festival of the Dead takes place, in which the city celebrates its rich cultural heritage through performances and art exhibitions. October and November are perfect for exploring the city at a slower pace, enjoying the art galleries, museums, and historical sites, all while experiencing Salamanca's cultural side in a more intimate way.

Winter (December to February)

Winter in Salamanca is cold but not extreme. The average temperatures during the winter months hover around 9-10°C (48-50°F) during the day, and it can dip to freezing or just above at night, especially in January. While snow is rare, you can expect crisp and chilly air, making it a good time to enjoy the city's indoor attractions, such as the museums, churches, and historic buildings. Winter visitors will find that Salamanca has a quiet, peaceful charm, as fewer tourists visit during this season.

December brings a festive atmosphere with the Christmas market in Plaza Mayor. This market offers an enchanting setting with Christmas lights, local handicrafts, food stalls, and seasonal decorations, creating a cozy ambiance perfect for a winter visit. If

26

you're in Salamanca for the holidays, New Year's Eve celebrations are also lively, with fireworks and public festivities in the central square to welcome the new year.

Though Salamanca is quieter in the winter months, it offers a more reflective experience, especially if you prefer to avoid large crowds. Visiting the city during winter also means lower accommodation costs and a more relaxed pace as you wander through the charming streets, sip hot beverages in cafés, and immerse yourself in the history of the place.

Weather Overview

Salamanca's climate is Mediterranean with continental influences, meaning the city experiences hot summers and cold winters. The city is located inland, which leads to temperature extremes between seasons. However, the weather is generally pleasant, and each season offers unique experiences for visitors.

Spring (March to May)

- **Average Daytime Temperatures**: 13-22°C (55-72°F)

- **Average Nighttime Temperatures**: 3-8°C (37-46°F)

- **Precipitation**: Moderate, with rain occurring intermittently throughout the season.

Spring is the most comfortable time to visit Salamanca, with mild temperatures and relatively dry weather. This season is ideal for outdoor activities and exploring the city's many attractions, from its historic squares to its academic institutions.

Summer (June to August)

- **Average Daytime Temperatures**: 27-31°C (81-88°F)

- **Average Nighttime Temperatures**: 16-18°C (61-64°F)

- **Precipitation**: Very little rainfall; mostly dry weather.

Summer is characterized by long days of sunshine and higher temperatures, which make it perfect for sightseeing but can become intense for those not accustomed to the heat. The city's outdoor cafes and terraces are especially popular during the summer months, offering the opportunity to relax and soak in the atmosphere while enjoying local cuisine.

Autumn (September to November)

- **Average Daytime Temperatures**: 13-25°C (55-77°F)

- **Average Nighttime Temperatures**: 5-13°C (41-55°F)

- **Precipitation**: Increased rainfall, especially in November.

Autumn is a beautiful time to visit Salamanca due to the changing foliage and cooler temperatures. The pleasant weather makes it an ideal time for walking tours, cultural festivals, and outdoor events. The city is also less crowded compared to the summer, making it a great time for a more peaceful and intimate experience.

Winter (December to February)

- **Average Daytime Temperatures**: 9-10°C (48-50°F)

- **Average Nighttime Temperatures**: 1-2°C (34-36°F)

- **Precipitation**: Light, with occasional rain or snow.

Winter is the coldest time of the year in Salamanca, but it is still quite manageable, with the lowest temperatures rarely dropping below freezing. The cooler weather, combined with fewer tourists, offers a more serene and relaxed atmosphere for those looking to explore the city's historical and cultural offerings.

Festivals and Events Throughout the Year

Salamanca is a city brimming with cultural life, and throughout the year, there are numerous festivals and events that highlight its rich traditions, arts, and history. Whether you visit in the spring for religious celebrations, in summer for vibrant arts festivals, or in winter for festive markets, there's always something to see and experience.

Spring Festivals

- **Semana Santa (Holy Week)**: One of the most significant religious celebrations in Spain, Semana Santa is observed in late March or early April. The processions through Salamanca's streets feature religious figures and elaborate floats, creating an emotional and awe-inspiring atmosphere. The processions, especially the one on Good Friday, are accompanied by hauntingly beautiful music and the sound of drums echoing through the streets.

- **Feria de Teatro (Theatre Fair)**: Held in May, this festival brings theatrical performances to Salamanca's stages, with both national and international troupes performing in theaters and public spaces. It's a wonderful way to experience the city's vibrant cultural scene.

Summer Festivals

- **International Arts Festival**: Held every July, this month-long festival celebrates a range of artistic expressions, from music and theater to dance and visual arts. Artists from all over the world participate, making Salamanca a global stage for creativity and innovation.

- **Feria de Salamanca**: This festival, celebrated in the summer, brings together the local community to honor the patron saint of Salamanca, La Virgen de la Vega. The festival features parades, live music, and fireworks, and it's a highlight for both locals and visitors.

Autumn Festivals

- **Festival of the Dead**: A fascinating blend of tradition and modernity, this October event celebrates the rich cultural heritage of the city with a mix of contemporary art exhibitions, performances, and public displays. It's a unique celebration of the city's artistic vitality and its deep historical roots.

- **Salamanca Fair**: A festival held in honor of the city's patron saint, La Virgen de la Vega, this event offers a wide range of activities, including concerts, fairs, and processions. It is a great opportunity to experience traditional Spanish festivities.

Winter Festivals

- **Christmas Market**: Salamanca's Christmas Market, held in Plaza Mayor during December, offers a magical setting for holiday shopping and festive cheer. With Christmas lights, seasonal treats, and artisan goods, it's an excellent time to experience the city's winter charm.

- **New Year's Eve Celebrations**: The Plaza Mayor hosts vibrant celebrations to ring in the new year. Fireworks, live music, and a festive atmosphere make Salamanca an exciting place to celebrate the transition into the new year.

The best time to visit Salamanca depends largely on your preferences, whether you're drawn to the cultural vibrancy of summer, the serene beauty of autumn, or the festive atmosphere of winter. Regardless of the season, Salamanca offers something for every traveler. Its rich history, stunning architecture, and lively festivals make it a wonderful destination year-round. Each season brings a different experience, from the warmth of spring flowers to the cool serenity of winter, ensuring that your visit will be memorable no matter when you choose to visit.

Chapter 4: Where to Stay in Salamanca

Salamanca, a city that blends historic charm with modern vibrancy, offers a wide range of accommodation options. Whether you're a luxury traveler, a budget-conscious backpacker, or someone in between, Salamanca has something to suit every need. This chapter takes you through the best places to stay, from high-end boutique hotels to budget-friendly hostels, ensuring that you find the perfect base for your stay in this beautiful Spanish city.

Recommended Hotels and Hostels

Salamanca is home to a variety of hotels and hostels that provide comfortable stays in central locations. Whether you're visiting for a few days or an extended stay, there are options that cater to different preferences and budgets.

1. Hotel Rector

Hotel Rector offers a refined and intimate experience. Located in the heart of Salamanca, it's a small, elegant boutique hotel where you'll enjoy a personalized experience. The hotel's decor is a seamless blend of classic Spanish style and modern amenities, creating an atmosphere of sophistication and comfort. With only 13 rooms, it ensures personalized attention and a peaceful stay in a city that's otherwise bustling with students and tourists. The staff's dedication to making each guest feel at home adds to the experience, and the hotel's location makes it ideal for exploring Salamanca's major attractions, like the University of Salamanca and Plaza Mayor.

2. Hotel Hospes Palacio de San Esteban

Set in a former convent, this five-star hotel is a perfect blend of history and luxury. The location is superb, just a short walk from the main attractions, such as the Old Cathedral and the University of Salamanca. The hotel offers an incredible sense of serenity, with a beautiful courtyard and cloisters where guests can unwind. The luxurious rooms, modern spa facilities, and gourmet dining at the restaurant provide an elevated stay. For those looking to explore the historic city with added comfort, this is a top-notch choice.

3. Soho Boutique Salamanca

For those who appreciate modern style with a central location, Soho Boutique Salamanca is an excellent option. It's situated near Plaza Mayor, which places visitors right in the middle of the action. The hotel boasts clean, contemporary rooms with plenty of natural light, making it a great place to relax after a day of sightseeing. Guests enjoy a range of services, including a full breakfast and attentive staff. If you're looking to stay in the heart of Salamanca's lively environment, this hotel will put you right where the action is.

4. Ibis Salamanca

The Ibis brand is known for offering affordable, no-frills accommodations without sacrificing comfort, and the Ibis Salamanca is no exception. It's conveniently located near the train station, making it a great choice for travelers arriving by rail. Rooms are simple but comfortable, and the staff is welcoming and helpful. If you're on a tight budget but still want easy access to the city's major attractions, this hotel offers great value for money.

5. Hostal Gud Salamanca

If you're looking for an affordable, family-run hostal with a central location, Hostal Gud Salamanca is an excellent choice. Just a short walk from Plaza Mayor, it offers clean rooms with essential amenities. The friendly staff and welcoming atmosphere make this hostal a great budget option for travelers who want to explore the city without breaking the bank.

Boutique and Luxury Options

For those seeking a more luxurious experience in Salamanca, several boutique and high-end hotels cater to discerning travelers. These properties combine exceptional service, exquisite design, and prime locations to ensure a memorable stay.

1. Grand Hotel Don Gregorio

Grand Hotel Don Gregorio offers a combination of history and luxury. Located in a beautifully restored 15th-century palace, this five-star property exudes old-world charm with its exquisite marble floors, antique furnishings, and grand chandeliers. The rooms are spacious and elegantly decorated, offering modern amenities in a historical setting. Guests can relax in the spa, enjoy fine dining at the on-site restaurant, or take a dip in the pool while admiring the views of the city's historic center. If you want to stay somewhere truly special in Salamanca, Grand Hotel Don Gregorio is a luxurious option that offers both comfort and historical allure.

2. Eunice Hotel Gastronómico

For travelers who enjoy good food alongside luxury accommodations, Eunice Hotel Gastronómico is an excellent choice. This boutique hotel emphasizes gastronomy, offering guests a chance to enjoy exquisite culinary experiences within a contemporary yet cozy environment. The design of the hotel is sleek and modern, with rooms offering elegant comfort and top-tier amenities. Whether you're indulging in a curated breakfast or enjoying dinner at the hotel's restaurant, Eunice Hotel Gastronómico promises to satisfy both your culinary cravings and your need for relaxation.

3. Hacienda Zorita Wine Hotel & Spa

Just outside Salamanca, Hacienda Zorita Wine Hotel & Spa offers a unique experience for wine lovers and those seeking a tranquil retreat. Set in a 700-year-old restored monastery along the Tormes River, the hotel is surrounded by picturesque vineyards. Guests can take part in wine tastings, explore the historic estate, and enjoy the luxurious amenities at the spa. The peaceful setting and top-notch services make it a fantastic place to relax after a day of sightseeing in Salamanca. If you're interested in experiencing the Spanish wine region, this hotel offers an immersive stay that combines luxury with the local heritage.

4. Castillo del Buen Amor

For a truly unique experience, consider staying at Castillo del Buen Amor, a luxury hotel set in a restored 15th-century castle. Located just outside the city, this spectacular property offers a truly royal experience. Surrounded by lush gardens and vineyards, the castle provides spacious rooms that blend medieval charm with modern luxury. Guests can enjoy wine tastings, dine in an elegant restaurant, and explore the nearby countryside. If you're looking for a romantic getaway or a special occasion retreat, this is the perfect place to unwind in style.

Budget-Friendly Accommodations

Travelers on a budget will find plenty of affordable options in Salamanca without compromising on comfort. From cozy hostels to more basic hotels, these accommodations provide great value for money and are perfect for those who prefer to spend their savings on experiences rather than high-end lodging.

1. Sercotel Las Torres Salamanca

Located just a short walk from Plaza Mayor, Sercotel Las Torres Salamanca is a three-star hotel offering great value for its location and amenities. The rooms are comfortable and well-equipped with essential amenities like free Wi-Fi, air conditioning, and a flat-screen TV. The hotel offers a delicious breakfast each morning, and its location makes it easy to explore the city's major attractions on foot. Sercotel Las Torres is an excellent choice for travelers who want to stay in a central location without spending a fortune.

2. Silken Rona Dalba

Silken Rona Dalba offers modern accommodations at affordable prices. Situated near the Old Town district, it's perfect for travelers who want to explore Salamanca's historic sites. The rooms are simple but clean and functional, with a range of amenities like free Wi-Fi and a television. With easy access to public transport and nearby attractions, Silken Rona Dalba is an ideal budget-friendly choice for those who want to stay close to the action without paying premium prices.

3. Hotel San Polo

Hotel San Polo is another excellent option for budget-conscious travelers. Located in a peaceful area near the Tormes River, the hotel offers spacious rooms and a friendly atmosphere. While it's a bit further from the heart of the historic district, it's still within walking distance of many attractions. The on-site restaurant serves local Spanish dishes, and guests can enjoy the relaxed ambiance of the hotel. It's perfect for families or solo travelers who want a good balance of comfort and affordability.

4. Salamanca Suite Studios

For a more independent stay, Salamanca Suite Studios offers fully equipped apartments for those who prefer self-catering accommodations. Located centrally, these studios allow you to experience Salamanca like a local. With kitchenettes, comfortable living spaces, and close proximity to the city's main attractions, these apartments are a great choice for longer stays or those who want the flexibility to prepare their own meals.

5. Emperatriz I

Emperatriz I is a 3-star hotel located in the shopping district of Salamanca. Its central location makes it convenient for travelers who want to be close to both the city's cultural sites and shopping options. The hotel offers modern, comfortable rooms at an affordable rate. Guests can enjoy free Wi-Fi, a restaurant serving Spanish cuisine, and easy access to transportation options. Emperatriz I is a practical, no-frills option for budget-conscious travelers who still want to enjoy the city's vibrant atmosphere.

Salamanca offers a variety of accommodations that cater to every type of traveler. From boutique hotels offering a unique experience to budget-friendly hostels and modern hotels, the city ensures that every visitor can find a comfortable place to stay while enjoying the beauty and history of this UNESCO World Heritage city. Whether you're visiting for a weekend getaway or a longer stay, you can be assured that your choice of accommodation will allow you to enjoy Salamanca to its fullest.

Chapter 5: Salamanca's Must-See Attractions

Salamanca is a city that is steeped in history and cultural richness. Its blend of medieval and Renaissance architecture, along with its vibrant student atmosphere, makes it one of Spain's most enchanting destinations. Whether you're an art enthusiast, a history lover, or simply someone seeking to experience the charm of this Spanish gem, there's something for everyone in Salamanca. In this chapter, we take a deeper look at the city's must-see attractions, including its iconic squares, world-renowned university, majestic cathedrals, and more.

Plaza Mayor

One of the most recognizable landmarks of Salamanca, Plaza Mayor is the heart of the city. This grand square is not only a significant historical site but also a social hub where locals and visitors gather to enjoy its beauty, cafés, and vibrant atmosphere. As one of the most stunning squares in Spain, Plaza Mayor has been an essential part of the city's identity for centuries.

The History of Plaza Mayor

The history of Plaza Mayor dates back to the 18th century, with its construction completed in 1756. It was designed by the architect Churriguera in the Baroque style, and its symmetry and grandeur have made it a prime example of Spanish public squares. Originally, the square was intended to host bullfights, public executions, and other events, with its open space serving as a central gathering place for the people of Salamanca. Over the centuries, it has evolved into a vibrant cultural and social hub.

Architectural Beauty

Plaza Mayor is an exceptional example of Baroque architecture, with its graceful arcades, grand stone facades, and detailed columns. The square is surrounded by three-story buildings, each adorned with intricate carvings, and features a central area that is both open and expansive. The square's design exudes a sense of harmony and grandeur, drawing the eye toward the central Casa de los Lemos and Casa de los Ovalle, which highlight the splendor of the square. Visitors can also see the 12 statues of Spanish kings, which are set into the building facades, adding a historical and artistic touch to the space.

A Social and Cultural Hub

Today, Plaza Mayor remains the city's focal point. It's the perfect spot to enjoy a coffee or tapas while people-watching. In the evenings, the square is lit up by the golden hue of its sandstone buildings, creating an enchanting atmosphere. Festivals, concerts, and events are often held here, making it a lively place to experience Salamanca's cultural life. Whether you're looking to relax or immerse yourself in the city's energy, Plaza Mayor offers a unique experience that perfectly encapsulates Salamanca's charm.

University of Salamanca

The University of Salamanca is one of the oldest and most prestigious universities in Europe. Established in 1218, it has long been a center for intellectual and academic activity, attracting students and scholars from around the world. This world-renowned institution has shaped the city's identity and continues to be one of its most visited attractions.

A Legacy of Learning

The University of Salamanca was founded by King Alfonso IX, who established the school with the purpose of promoting education and learning. Over the centuries, it has grown to become an internationally recognized center for higher education. Throughout its history, the university has produced numerous notable alumni, including poets, writers, philosophers, and scientists. It has also played a significant role in shaping Spanish language and literature, contributing to Spain's rich cultural and intellectual heritage.

The university's most famous figure is Fray Luis de León, a poet, theologian, and mystic. His work continues to be studied today, and his influence on the development of Spanish literature is immeasurable. The university also has connections to Christopher Columbus, as it was here that he presented his proposal for the discovery of the New World.

Architectural Splendor

The University of Salamanca is a masterpiece of architectural beauty. The Plaza del Abogado and the Escuelas Mayores (Main School) are among the most striking buildings, showcasing the university's grandeur. The intricate Plateresque façade of the Escuelas Mayores is a true work of art, featuring a combination of Renaissance and Gothic styles. Visitors are often drawn to the façade's ornate decorations, including the famous "frog on a skull" carving. This hidden detail has become a symbol of the university, and it's said that if you spot the frog, you will gain good luck.

The Library of the University is also worth a visit, with its impressive collection of rare manuscripts and books. The university continues to be a center of education and research, and its historic buildings are a testament to its long and storied history.

The Old and New Cathedrals

Salamanca's cathedrals are among the most important landmarks in the city. The Old Cathedral and New Cathedral stand side by side, offering a fascinating juxtaposition of Romanesque and

Gothic styles that reflect the city's architectural and religious evolution.

The Old Cathedral (Catedral Vieja)

Dating back to the 12th century, the Old Cathedral is a beautiful example of Romanesque architecture. Its tower dominates the Salamanca skyline, and the cathedral itself is a symbol of the city's medieval past. Inside, visitors are treated to stunning works of art, including frescoes, sculptures, and intricate stained-glass windows that depict biblical stories. One of the most fascinating aspects of the Old Cathedral is its mysterious Romanesque crypt, which is said to have been the site of religious rituals for centuries.

The altar in the Old Cathedral is a masterpiece of medieval craftsmanship, with its elaborate carvings and religious iconography that highlight the devotion and faith of the era. The building's walls are adorned with stunning frescoes, depicting saints and biblical scenes that tell the story of the Christian faith through the ages.

The New Cathedral (Catedral Nueva)

Built between the 16th and 18th centuries, the New Cathedral showcases a blend of Gothic, Baroque, and Renaissance styles. The New Cathedral's towering spires and impressive façade stand as a testament to the city's religious significance. The cathedral's interior is equally magnificent, with high vaulted ceilings, intricate carvings, and impressive altarpieces.

One of the highlights of the New Cathedral is the Golden Chapel, which is filled with beautiful sculptures and works of art. The cloister of the New Cathedral is another must-see, offering visitors a peaceful space to admire the architecture and the tranquil surroundings.

The organ of the New Cathedral is one of the most renowned in Spain, and its music echoes throughout the cathedral during special religious services. For those interested in learning about the history of the cathedrals, guided tours are available, offering insights into the art, architecture, and religious significance of these stunning buildings.

Casa de las Conchas

Located just a short walk from Plaza Mayor, the Casa de las Conchas is one of Salamanca's most iconic buildings. This 15th-century mansion, whose name translates to "House of Shells," is known for its distinctive façade, which is adorned with over 300 scallop shells. These shells are thought to symbolize the owner's connection to the Order of Santiago, an ancient Spanish military and religious order.

A Fascinating Building

The Casa de las Conchas was originally built as a noble residence for Rodrigo Arias de Maldonado, a wealthy and influential figure in Salamanca's 15th-century society. The building's design reflects the architectural style of the time, blending Gothic and Renaissance elements. The shells that decorate the exterior are not just ornamental; they also serve as a reminder of the building's connection to the Order of Santiago, which granted privileges to those who wore the shell as their emblem.

Inside, visitors will find a courtyard that is just as charming as the exterior. The arcades around the courtyard and the staircase that leads to the upper floors are beautifully crafted and offer a glimpse into the past. The building now houses a public library and a cultural center, making it a significant part of Salamanca's intellectual and artistic life.

Palacio de Anaya

The Palacio de Anaya is another architectural gem in Salamanca, located near the University of Salamanca. This impressive palace, with its grand façade and ornate details, is a beautiful example of Baroque architecture. The palace was originally constructed in the 16th century and has been home to various noble families over the centuries.

The Architecture

The Palacio de Anaya is particularly known for its elegant façade, which is adorned with intricate carvings and classical columns. The building's stonework and symmetry are characteristic of the Baroque style, and its doorways and windows are framed with detailed decorations that reflect the city's wealth and cultural significance during the Renaissance.

Visitors can explore the courtyard, which is one of the most striking features of the palace. The arches and staircases lead to the upper floors, where many of the palace's rooms are now used for exhibitions and public events. Today, the palace houses the School of Law of the University of Salamanca, which makes it an important part of the university's legacy.

The Clerecía Church

The Clerecía Church (Iglesia de la Clerecía) is a monumental Baroque church located near the Universidad Pontificia de Salamanca. It was built in the 17th century as a Jesuit church and is known for its magnificent facade and interior. The church was part of a larger religious complex, which included a Jesuit seminary and monastery.

An Architectural Masterpiece

The Clerecía Church's façade is a striking example of Baroque architecture, with intricate carvings, towers, and statues that depict various saints and religious figures. The church's interior is equally impressive, with a high, vaulted ceiling and beautiful paintings that adorn the walls. The altar is made from marble, with detailed carvings and gilded accents that give it a sense of grandeur.

Visitors can also explore the tower of the Clerecía Church, which offers stunning panoramic views of the city. The church's rich history, impressive architecture, and religious significance make it a must-see for anyone visiting Salamanca.

Salamanca's must-see attractions, including Plaza Mayor, the University of Salamanca, the Old and New Cathedrals, Casa de las Conchas, Palacio de Anaya, and the Clerecía Church, offer a rich and varied experience for visitors. Whether you're marveling at the grandeur of Salamanca's architecture, exploring its historic sites, or simply soaking in the vibrant atmosphere, these landmarks provide an unforgettable glimpse into the city's history, culture, and heritage. Each attraction offers a unique perspective on the city's past and present, ensuring that every visitor leaves with a deeper appreciation of this beautiful Spanish gem.

Chapter 6: Exploring Salamanca's Historic Center

Salamanca's Historic Center is one of the most well-preserved and charming old towns in Spain, offering an unmatched opportunity to experience the city's cultural and architectural heritage. From its ancient streets and vibrant plazas to its stunning buildings and secret courtyards, Salamanca invites travelers to walk through centuries of history, discovering the stories that have shaped this beautiful city. This chapter takes you on a detailed journey through Salamanca's Historic Center, with a focus on walking tours, its unique architecture and landmarks, hidden gems, and secret courtyards and plazas.

Walking Tours

Salamanca's Historic Center is best explored on foot. Walking through the narrow streets and alleys allows you to absorb the city's charm at a leisurely pace, giving you time to appreciate the architecture, soak in the atmosphere, and stumble upon hidden gems along the way. Many of Salamanca's most famous attractions, such as Plaza Mayor, the University of Salamanca, and the Cathedrals, are located within walking distance of each other, making it easy to explore the heart of the city on foot.

Guided Walking Tours

For those looking to make the most of their time and gain deeper insights into Salamanca's rich history, guided walking tours are a great option. Local guides, often passionate about their city's history, lead visitors through the labyrinth of streets that make up the Historic Center. These tours typically begin in the Plaza Mayor, where guides provide an overview of the city's past and introduce visitors to the most significant landmarks.

Guided walking tours in Salamanca often cover the city's most iconic sites, including the University of Salamanca, Casa de las Conchas, and La Clerecía Church. Visitors are given detailed explanations about the history, architecture, and cultural significance of each site. Guides often share stories about the city's medieval past, the golden age of Spanish literature, and the intellectual legacy of the University of Salamanca. Walking tours usually last between one and two hours, offering a deep dive into the city's culture and history.

Self-Guided Walking Tours

For those who prefer to explore independently, a self-guided walking tour is also a great option. The city's compact size and pedestrian-friendly streets make it easy to navigate on your own.

Many tourists choose to follow a suggested walking route, starting from Plaza Mayor, the city's most famous square, and making their way to nearby attractions. Along the way, visitors can explore the city's medieval walls, picturesque streets, and beautiful buildings at their own pace.

Salamanca's Historic Center is home to numerous landmarks, many of which are concentrated in the heart of the city. One self-guided walking route might take you from Plaza Mayor, through the Calle Toro, and up to the University of Salamanca, with stops at Casa de las Conchas, the Old Cathedral, and the New Cathedral. This walking tour would allow you to explore Salamanca's architectural evolution, from Romanesque to Baroque, while learning about the city's role in Spanish history and culture.

Architecture and Landmarks

Salamanca's Historic Center is a showcase of architectural beauty. From medieval structures to Renaissance and Baroque masterpieces, the city's landmarks reflect its rich history, academic heritage, and artistic legacy. As you explore the center, you will encounter a variety of architectural styles, each telling its own story about the city's past.

Plaza Mayor

The Plaza Mayor is undoubtedly the jewel of Salamanca's Historic Center. Designed in the Baroque style, the square was completed in 1756 and serves as the heart of the city. Its harmonious design is characterized by a rectangular shape, with three-story buildings surrounding the square. The buildings are made of sandstone, which gives the square a warm, golden hue that becomes even more striking at sunset. The square is adorned with 12 statues of Spanish kings, adding a regal touch to the space.

Throughout history, Plaza Mayor has been a place for both celebration and reflection. In the 18th century, it hosted bullfights, public executions, and festivals. Today, it is a vibrant social space, with cafés, restaurants, and bars lining the edges. The square is the perfect place to sit and people-watch, while soaking in the beauty of the surroundings.

University of Salamanca

The University of Salamanca is one of the oldest and most prestigious universities in Europe, founded in 1218. The Escuelas Mayores, the university's main building, is a striking example of Plateresque architecture and is often considered one of the finest examples of Spanish Renaissance architecture. The intricate carvings on the façade of the Escuelas Mayores include biblical scenes, religious figures, and mythological creatures, showcasing the skill of the craftsmen who worked on the building.

The university is not only an architectural marvel but also a cultural institution of immense importance. The Frog on the Skull carving on the facade of Escuelas Mayores is perhaps the most famous detail, with visitors seeking it out as part of the tradition to bring them good luck. The university also houses one of the oldest libraries in Europe, where many rare manuscripts and books are preserved.

The Cathedrals: Old and New

Salamanca is home to two stunning cathedrals, the Old Cathedral and the New Cathedral, which are located side by side in the heart of the city. The Old Cathedral, built in the 12th century, is a remarkable example of Romanesque architecture. It is known for its impressive frescoes and crypt, which add to its mysterious allure.

In contrast, the New Cathedral was built between the 16th and 18th centuries and is a magnificent example of Gothic and Baroque styles. The cathedral's soaring spires and grand interior, with its ornate altar and intricate stained-glass windows, are awe-inspiring. One of the cathedral's most famous features is the Golden Chapel, a stunning display of Baroque craftsmanship.

Together, these two cathedrals represent Salamanca's spiritual and architectural evolution, from the medieval to the modern.

Casa de las Conchas

The Casa de las Conchas (House of Shells) is one of Salamanca's most distinctive buildings, known for its façade covered in over 300 scallop shells. The shells are believed to be symbols of the Order of Santiago, and their inclusion on the building's façade adds an air of mystery to the otherwise simple building. The mansion, built in the late 15th century, is an excellent example of Plateresque architecture, a style that combines Gothic and Renaissance elements.

Today, the Casa de las Conchas houses a public library, and visitors can explore the building's grand courtyard and staircase. The building is located near Plaza Mayor, making it an easy stop for anyone walking through the city center.

Hidden Gems in the Old City

Salamanca's Historic Center is filled with well-known landmarks, but there are also plenty of hidden gems tucked away in the city's winding streets. These lesser-known spots provide an opportunity to explore the more intimate side of the city.

The Clerecía Church

While the Clerecía Church may not be as famous as the Cathedrals, it is still an architectural gem that deserves attention. Located near the Universidad Pontificia de Salamanca, the church is a magnificent example of Baroque design. Its towering façade is adorned with intricate carvings of religious figures, and the church's interior is just as impressive, with a high vaulted ceiling and ornate altarpieces.

One of the best-kept secrets of the Clerecía Church is its tower, which offers stunning views over the city and the surrounding countryside. It's a hidden spot that many visitors overlook, but it provides one of the best panoramic views in Salamanca.

Calle Tentenecio

For a peaceful, picturesque experience, head to Calle Tentenecio, a narrow street in the Old City that is filled with traditional Spanish buildings. Lined with vibrant flowers and charming little shops, this street is a lovely spot for a quiet walk. The street leads to the Plaza de los Bandos, a charming square that is often overlooked by tourists. It's a perfect place to take a break, enjoy a coffee, and watch the world go by.

Puente Romano (Roman Bridge)

The Puente Romano, or Roman Bridge, is an ancient structure that spans the Tormes River, offering a scenic route into the city. While the bridge itself is a well-known landmark, many visitors miss the chance to walk along its stone path and enjoy the view of the river and surrounding area. The bridge is especially beautiful at sunset, when the light reflects off the river and creates a stunning backdrop for photos.

Secret Courtyards and Plazas

One of the most enchanting aspects of Salamanca's Historic Center is its collection of hidden courtyards and plazas. These peaceful spots are often tucked behind facades, offering visitors a serene escape from the bustling streets of the city.

Plaza de la Libertad

A lesser-known but charming square, Plaza de la Libertad is located just off the main tourist route. Surrounded by charming cafes and historical buildings, this square offers a quiet place to relax and enjoy the beauty of Salamanca without the crowds. The square is often overlooked by tourists, making it the perfect spot to enjoy a peaceful moment away from the hustle and bustle.

The Cloisters of the University

The Cloisters of the University of Salamanca are often missed by tourists in favor of the more famous attractions. However, these beautiful spaces, with their serene gardens and intricate stonework, are a true hidden gem. Visitors can walk through the peaceful courtyards, enjoy the quiet atmosphere, and take in the beauty of the Renaissance architecture.

Salamanca's Historic Center is a treasure trove of architectural wonders, hidden gems, and tranquil spaces waiting to be discovered. From the grandeur of its cathedrals and university to the quiet charm of its lesser-known streets and plazas, there is no shortage of beauty and history to explore. Whether you're strolling through the bustling Plaza Mayor, walking along the ancient Roman Bridge, or discovering a secret courtyard tucked away behind a grand building, Salamanca offers a unique opportunity to step back in time and immerse yourself in the city's rich cultural heritage. A walk through Salamanca's Historic Center is not just a tour – it's an experience that will stay with you long after you've left the city.

Chapter 7: Salamanca's Best Restaurants and Cafés

Salamanca is not only a feast for the eyes with its stunning architecture and rich history but also a haven for food lovers. The city's culinary scene is a celebration of traditional Spanish flavors, with a vibrant tapas culture, a growing focus on vegetarian and vegan options, and a range of sweet treats that reflect the local culture. Whether you're looking to dive into a hearty traditional Spanish meal, savor a small plate of tapas with a glass of wine, or enjoy a peaceful coffee in one of Salamanca's charming cafés, this chapter will guide you through the best culinary experiences the city has to offer.

Traditional Spanish Cuisine

When visiting Salamanca, one of the first things you'll notice is the emphasis on traditional Spanish cuisine, deeply rooted in the region's agricultural and cultural history. From hearty stews to flavorful meats, the food here is rich, satisfying, and full of history. As a city that prides itself on its culinary heritage, Salamanca offers an abundance of restaurants that showcase the best of

Castilian cuisine, particularly dishes that have been passed down through generations.

Cochinillo Asado (Roast Suckling Pig)

One of the quintessential dishes of Salamanca and the wider Castile and León region is cochinillo asado, or roast suckling pig. This dish features a tender, melt-in-your-mouth piglet that is slow-cooked to perfection until its skin is crispy and golden. The preparation requires a delicate balance of seasoning and slow roasting, ensuring that the meat is tender while the skin retains its crispy texture. Many traditional restaurants in Salamanca serve this dish, particularly in the La Alamedilla and Plaza Mayor areas.

Some of the best spots to try cochinillo asado include Restaurante Zaramama, known for its elegant take on classic Castilian dishes, and La Cocina de Toño, where the roast pig is served alongside other traditional dishes like judiones de la granja (a type of large white beans stew) and ensalada de pimientos.

Chuletón de Buey (T-Bone Steak)

Another beloved dish in Salamanca is the chuletón de buey, a large T-bone steak often grilled to perfection. This dish showcases the region's famous beef, and it is typically served with a simple accompaniment of patatas fritas (fried potatoes) or a side salad. The meat is typically seasoned with just salt and pepper, allowing the quality of the beef to shine through. At Restaurante El

Alquimista, diners can enjoy a perfectly cooked chuletón de buey, where the meat is served sizzling, allowing you to enjoy it at your own pace.

Hornazo (Meat Pie)

A classic regional specialty, hornazo is a savory meat pie filled with pork, chorizo, and hard-boiled eggs, encased in a flaky, golden pastry. Hornazo is traditionally enjoyed during the Easter season but can be found year-round in many restaurants and bakeries. One of the most famous places to try hornazo in Salamanca is El Molino de la Vega, a local bakery that has been making the traditional pie for decades. You'll often find hornazo served as a snack or a light lunch, enjoyed with a cold beer or a glass of local wine.

Tapas Bars and Wine Spots

Salamanca is a city where tapas culture thrives, with countless bars and taverns offering small, flavorful dishes that pair perfectly with a glass of wine. The art of tapas is an integral part of daily life in the city, and visitors can indulge in a variety of small plates that showcase the region's local ingredients and culinary creativity. Salamanca's tapas bars and wine spots offer an authentic taste of Spain, where locals and tourists alike can enjoy a casual yet memorable dining experience.

Bar Cielo

One of the most popular tapas spots in Salamanca is Bar Cielo, located just off Plaza Mayor. Known for its intimate setting and exceptional service, this tapas bar offers a menu that focuses on local delicacies. The jamón ibérico de bellota (acorn-fed Iberian ham) is a must-try, as it pairs beautifully with a glass of ribeiro or verdejo, two wines that hail from the Castilla y León region. The selection of cheeses, including manchego and cabra, also adds to the charm of the place. Whether you're enjoying a pre-dinner glass of wine or indulging in a full tapas experience, Bar Cielo provides a quintessential Salamanca tapas experience.

La Taberna del Loco

Another standout tapas bar is La Taberna del Loco, a favorite among both locals and visitors. This lively spot offers an array of creative tapas that combine traditional Spanish flavors with modern twists. Their tuna tartare served with wasabi mayo and their signature patatas bravas—fried potatoes with spicy tomato sauce and aioli—are crowd favorites. Alongside tapas, the bar offers a robust wine list, with local Castilian wines that perfectly complement the tapas offerings.

Vinodiario

If you're looking for a more sophisticated wine experience, Vinodiario is the place to be. This wine bar offers an impressive selection of local and international wines, paired with a carefully curated menu of tapas. The owners have a deep love for Spanish wine, and their knowledge is evident in the way they guide guests through their selection. Their tasting menus, which pair wine with an array of regional tapas, provide an unforgettable experience for both wine connoisseurs and casual drinkers alike.

Vegetarian and Vegan Options

While traditional Spanish cuisine is often meat-heavy, Salamanca has seen a growing number of restaurants offering vegetarian and vegan options. Whether you're looking for plant-based versions of traditional dishes or innovative vegan creations, the city offers a range of eateries that cater to those with dietary preferences. Salamanca's chefs are increasingly incorporating local vegetables, legumes, and grains into their menus, providing satisfying and flavorful options for vegetarians and vegans alike.

Café de Lis

A popular spot for vegetarians and vegans is Café de Lis, a cozy and inviting café that focuses on plant-based cuisine. Their menu includes fresh salads, sandwiches, and vegan tapas, all made from locally sourced ingredients. The vegan burgers made from chickpeas and quinoa are a crowd favorite, as is their vegan paella, which uses seasonal vegetables and saffron to create a satisfying dish. The café also offers a range of organic teas and fresh juices, making it the perfect spot for a light, health-conscious meal.

La Hoja 21

For those seeking a more contemporary dining experience, La Hoja 21 offers innovative vegetarian and vegan dishes in an elegant setting. Located just outside the city center, the restaurant prides itself on using seasonal vegetables and plant-based proteins to create dishes that are both delicious and sustainable. Their signature vegan risotto, made with wild mushrooms and truffle oil, is a hit among regulars. The restaurant also offers a rotating vegetarian tasting menu that pairs well with a selection of Spanish wines.

D'Rafael

Another excellent vegan-friendly restaurant is D'Rafael, located in the heart of Salamanca. This vibrant eatery specializes in plant-based versions of classic Spanish dishes like vegan tortilla española (Spanish omelette) and vegan paella. The restaurant also offers an array of salads, sandwiches, and tapas that make it a go-to spot for vegans in the city. Their vegan churros, served with a rich, dark chocolate dipping sauce, are a delightful treat.

Local Sweets and Desserts to Try

No visit to Salamanca is complete without indulging in some of the city's local sweets and desserts. From traditional Spanish pastries to regional specialties, the city offers a delightful array of sugary treats that will satisfy any sweet tooth.

Tarta de Santiago

One of the most famous desserts in Salamanca is Tarta de Santiago, an almond cake that is popular throughout Spain. This moist cake is made with ground almonds, sugar, and eggs, creating a rich and nutty flavor. Traditionally, the cake is topped with the Cross of Saint James, a symbol of the pilgrimage to Santiago de Compostela. It is often served with a dollop of whipped cream or a scoop of vanilla ice cream. You can find Tarta de Santiago at many local bakeries, but Pastelería La Suiza is a top choice for its perfectly executed version of the dessert.

Flan de Queso (Cheese Flan)

A favorite in Salamanca, Flan de Queso is a local variation of the traditional Spanish flan, made with cheese to create a creamy and rich texture. This dessert is often served chilled and is typically garnished with caramel sauce. The cheesecake-like consistency of the flan de queso sets it apart from regular flan, making it a must-try treat for anyone with a sweet tooth. Many traditional restaurants in Salamanca, such as Restaurante El Alquimista, serve this dessert as part of their menu.

Churros y Chocolate

For a truly Spanish dessert experience, head to a churrería in Salamanca. Churros y chocolate is a quintessential Spanish treat: deep-fried dough sticks served with a thick, rich chocolate sauce for dipping. Whether you enjoy churros for breakfast, an afternoon snack, or dessert, they are a popular indulgence in

Salamanca. One of the best places to enjoy this indulgence is Churrería La Antigua, where the churros are hot, crispy, and perfect for dipping.

Best Coffee Spots in Salamanca

For coffee lovers, Salamanca is home to several excellent cafés, ranging from quaint, family-run spots to sleek, modern establishments. The city's café culture is thriving, offering a variety of brews, from strong **café con leche** to refreshing iced coffees. Whether you're looking for a quiet place to relax or a vibrant café to enjoy a drink with friends, Salamanca has you covered.

Café Novelty

One of the oldest and most beloved coffee spots in Salamanca is Café Novelty, a historic café that dates back to 1905. Located in Plaza Mayor, it is the perfect place to sip a coffee while enjoying the view of the square. Café Novelty serves a range of high-quality coffee blends, including espresso, café con leche, and cortado, all made from freshly ground beans. The café is also famous for its tarta de queso and other pastries, making it an excellent spot for breakfast or an afternoon treat.

Moka Coffee

For those seeking a modern, trendy atmosphere, Moka Coffee is a must-visit. Located in the city center, Moka Coffee specializes in high-quality beans and offers a variety of coffee drinks, from traditional espresso-based beverages to creative iced coffee concoctions. The café has a cozy ambiance with plenty of natural light, perfect for a relaxing break. Moka Coffee also offers light snacks and pastries, making it a great place to catch up with friends or relax after a day of sightseeing.

Café de Lis

Café de Lis offers a more laid-back, bohemian vibe, making it a favorite among students and locals. Located near the University of Salamanca, the café serves organic, fair-trade coffee and a selection of teas. The café's charming interior, complete with mismatched furniture and eclectic décor, makes it a cozy spot to unwind. Café de Lis also offers a selection of healthy snacks and cakes, including vegan-friendly options.

Salamanca's dining scene offers something for everyone. From its rich tradition of Spanish cuisine to the lively tapas bars and innovative vegan restaurants, there's no shortage of culinary delights to explore. Whether you're savoring a hearty Castilian dish, indulging in a sweet tarta de Santiago, or sipping a perfect cup of coffee in a historic café, Salamanca invites you to immerse yourself in its vibrant food culture.

Chapter 8: Shopping in Salamanca

Salamanca is a city that offers more than just historical and cultural experiences—it also boasts a thriving shopping scene that caters to a wide variety of tastes. Whether you are on the hunt for unique souvenirs, traditional crafts, high-end fashion, or vintage treasures, Salamanca has it all. The city's shopping experience is a wonderful blend of modern retail outlets, traditional markets, and artisan workshops, providing an unforgettable shopping adventure. This chapter will guide you through the best places to shop in Salamanca, from local crafts to designer stores, as well as the markets and antique shops that make this city a hidden shopping gem.

Souvenirs and Local Crafts

One of the joys of shopping in Salamanca is the opportunity to take home a piece of the city's culture and heritage. The shops specializing in souvenirs and local crafts offer an array of items that celebrate the city's rich traditions, whether through handmade pottery, leather goods, or local textiles. These souvenirs are not only a perfect reminder of your visit but also support local artisans and their craftsmanship.

Ceramics and Pottery

Salamanca has a long history of producing high-quality ceramics and pottery, and you'll find many shops in the city offering traditional handcrafted pieces. The city's ceramics are known for their vibrant colors, intricate designs, and unique charm. Many of these pieces feature traditional motifs, such as sunflowers, geometric patterns, and local symbols. These ceramics make wonderful souvenirs, whether you choose to buy decorative items like vases, plates, and bowls or functional pieces such as mugs and pitchers.

One of the most prominent stores to buy ceramics is Cerámica Salmantina. Located in the historic center, this shop offers a wide selection of traditional Spanish pottery, with each piece showcasing the distinctive style and craftsmanship of the region. The Alfarería de La Abuela is another great place, offering a range of handcrafted ceramic pieces made by local artisans.

Leather Goods

Leather craftsmanship is another proud tradition in Salamanca, and there are plenty of shops where you can find leather goods made from high-quality materials. From bags and wallets to belts and jackets, Salamanca's leather artisans create beautiful, durable products. The leather items in these shops are often handmade, giving each product a unique character.

A standout shop for leather goods is Piel Salamanca, a family-owned business that specializes in handcrafted leather accessories. Here, you can purchase beautifully crafted leather bags, belts, wallets, and even jackets, all of which are made using traditional techniques. If you're looking for something a bit more custom, the store offers personalized leather engraving to add your initials or a special message to any item.

Textiles and Embroidery

Salamanca's textile crafts are also notable, with intricate embroidery and woven fabrics being a significant part of the city's artistic tradition. The textiles here are often handwoven or hand-embroidered, making them unique and one-of-a-kind. Scarves, tablecloths, and pillow covers made from wool and linen are popular purchases, as are traditional shawls and woven baskets.

La Casa de la Seda offers an array of finely crafted silk scarves, purses, and shawls, which are made using traditional methods that have been passed down through generations. These items are ideal for anyone looking for a souvenir that reflects the skill and creativity of Salamanca's textile artisans.

Fashion and Designer Stores

For those looking for more modern or luxury shopping experiences, Salamanca offers a wide range of fashion stores, from well-known Spanish brands to international designer labels. The city's shopping districts are filled with chic boutiques and high-end retailers, offering a diverse mix of styles, trends, and high-quality merchandise.

Calle Toro

Calle Toro is one of the most famous shopping streets in Salamanca, offering a mix of high-street fashion and boutique stores. This pedestrian-friendly street is lined with an array of shops, making it the perfect place to spend a few hours shopping. The street is home to several Spanish brands, including Zara, Mango, and Massimo Dutti, which are known for their stylish and affordable fashion collections.

If you're looking for something a bit more luxurious, the street also has high-end boutiques and designer stores where you can find items from international brands such as Gucci, Louis Vuitton, and Prada. Calle Toro has a great mix of both modern fashion and classic styles, making it the perfect place for a shopping spree.

Calle de la Rúa

For more unique fashion finds, Calle de la Rúa is another popular shopping street in Salamanca. This area is home to smaller, independent fashion boutiques, offering everything from stylish women's clothing to trendy streetwear. The stores here cater to a younger crowd, with more experimental and artistic pieces that reflect the vibrant student culture of the city.

If you're looking for handmade accessories, jewelry, or contemporary clothing, this street has several shops worth visiting. One such boutique is La Trastienda, a well-known spot for fashionable clothing and eclectic accessories.

Markets and Shopping Streets

Salamanca has several lively markets and shopping streets where you can find everything from fresh produce to artisanal products. These markets provide a chance to experience the local culture and pick up unique items that reflect the spirit of the city.

Mercado Central

The Mercado Central (Central Market) is a bustling market where locals shop for fresh produce, meats, cheeses, and other foodstuffs. The market is housed in a beautiful building that dates back to the early 20th century, and it has a lively atmosphere that reflects the city's culinary culture. While the market is known for its food, it's also a great place to find local crafts, including handmade baskets, pottery, and textiles.

One of the highlights of the Mercado Central is the section dedicated to local cheeses and cured meats, where you can sample the region's famous jamón ibérico (Iberian ham) and queso manchego (Manchego cheese). It's an ideal spot to purchase local products to take home or enjoy a quick bite at one of the market's food stalls.

Mercado de San Juan de la Cruz

The Mercado de San Juan de la Cruz is another wonderful market in Salamanca, known for its range of local products and handmade goods. This market has a more artisan feel, and it's the perfect place to find unique souvenirs, such as handcrafted jewelry, wooden sculptures, and paintings by local artists. The market is located just outside the city center, making it an ideal spot to explore if you're looking to experience the more authentic side of Salamanca's shopping scene.

Calle de Compañía

Calle de Compañía is one of the city's most famous shopping streets, offering a wide range of stores, from local shops to international retailers. This street is particularly known for its fashion boutiques and artisanal goods, making it a great place for those who are looking to explore both high-end and handmade options. The street is also home to some of Salamanca's cafés and restaurants, so after a day of shopping, it's the perfect spot to relax and enjoy a meal or drink.

Antique Shops and Local Artisans

For those in search of something truly unique, Salamanca is also home to antique shops and local artisans who specialize in crafting one-of-a-kind items. From vintage furniture to hand-carved sculptures, these stores offer a glimpse into Salamanca's past, providing treasures that reflect the city's cultural and artistic heritage.

Antigüedades Abadía

One of the top antique shops in the city is Antigüedades Abadía, located near the city center. This family-owned shop specializes in vintage furniture, artwork, and collectibles, making it an excellent destination for those looking for rare, historical pieces. Whether you're searching for antique mirrors, old books, or unique sculptures, Antigüedades Abadía has a diverse selection of items that are perfect for collectors or anyone seeking a special souvenir from their trip.

Galería San Esteban

For those interested in local art, Galería San Esteban is a gallery and artisan shop that features works by Salamanca's finest local artists. From paintings and sculptures to handmade ceramics and jewelry, this gallery showcases a variety of works that reflect the city's artistic culture. The gallery also offers a selection of contemporary art, providing visitors with the chance to bring home something truly unique.

Alfarería La Abuela

For traditional Spanish craftsmanship, Alfarería La Abuela is an excellent place to visit. Specializing in handmade pottery, this charming shop offers an array of beautifully crafted ceramic pieces, including vases, plates, and bowls, many of which feature traditional designs that have been passed down through generations. Each piece is made using techniques that have been refined over centuries, and the shop's warm and inviting atmosphere adds to the experience.

Salamanca's shopping scene is a delightful mix of modern and traditional, offering a wide range of options for every kind of shopper. Whether you're looking for local crafts, fashion, antiques, or handmade goods, the city's markets, boutiques, and artisan shops provide a unique shopping experience that reflects the cultural richness of the region. Salamanca is a city where you can find beautiful souvenirs to remember your trip, high-end fashion for those seeking luxury, and rare treasures for collectors. Every corner of the city offers something special, making shopping in Salamanca a memorable part of your visit.

Chapter 9: Day Trips from Salamanca

Salamanca, with its stunning architecture and rich cultural heritage, offers plenty to see and do within the city itself. However, the surrounding region, Castilla y León, is equally fascinating, with charming towns, picturesque villages, dramatic landscapes, and a wealth of history and nature waiting to be explored. This chapter takes you on a journey through some of the best day trips from Salamanca, including nearby countryside, historical towns, adventure activities, and more. Whether you're looking to explore hidden gems or enjoy outdoor adventures, the area surrounding Salamanca has something for everyone.

Exploring the Surrounding Countryside

Castilla y León, where Salamanca is located, is known for its vast and varied countryside that ranges from rolling plains and broad rivers to rugged hills and forests. The region's natural beauty makes it an ideal destination for outdoor enthusiasts and anyone looking to escape into nature.

Sierra de Francia

One of the most beautiful areas close to Salamanca is the Sierra de Francia, a mountainous region located to the south of the city. This area is part of the Arribes del Duero Natural Park, offering a stunning backdrop of jagged peaks, deep gorges, and lush forests. It's perfect for those who enjoy hiking, wildlife watching, or simply immersing themselves in the serene atmosphere of the mountains.

La Alberca, a picturesque village in the heart of the Sierra de Francia, is a highlight of this region. A UNESCO heritage site, La Alberca is known for its well-preserved medieval architecture, cobbled streets, and traditional homes made from stone and wood. It's a perfect place to experience the charm of rural Spain, with many visitors also choosing to hike in the nearby hills or visit the natural parks surrounding the village.

If you enjoy a slower pace, the village of Mogarraz offers a wonderful escape. Known for its traditional houses and breathtaking landscapes, it offers visitors a chance to experience the rural life of Castilla y León. Many of the homes here still carry the traditional craftsmanship that has been passed down through generations.

Castilla y León's Vineyards

Another aspect of the surrounding countryside that visitors can explore is the wine regions. Castilla y León is one of Spain's premier wine-producing areas, with several regions famous for their wines, such as the Ribera del Duero, Rueda, and Toro. A visit to these regions allows you to experience the vineyards, wineries, and wine tasting tours that are part of the area's rich agricultural heritage.

Nearby Towns and Villages Worth Visiting

While Salamanca itself is packed with history and charm, there are many nearby towns and villages that are worth exploring. Each of these destinations offers a unique glimpse into the culture, history, and lifestyle of rural Castilla y León. From small medieval villages to larger historical towns, these day trips make for unforgettable experiences.

Ávila

One of the most famous day trips from Salamanca is a visit to the historical city of Ávila, located about 110 kilometers west of Salamanca. Known as the City of Saints and Stone, Ávila is famous for its medieval walls, which are among the best-preserved in Europe. These walls, built between the 11th and 14th centuries, are an extraordinary feat of engineering and architecture, stretching for over 2.5 kilometers and encircling the city.

Aside from the iconic walls, Ávila is home to many other historical sites, including the Cathedral of Ávila, a stunning example of Romanesque and Gothic architecture, and Santa Teresa de Jesús convent, dedicated to the famous mystic and reformer, Saint Teresa. The Plaza Mayor of Ávila is the perfect spot to sit and enjoy the atmosphere of the town while taking in the view of the impressive city walls.

In addition to its religious and historical significance, Ávila is known for its marzipan, a local sweet that you can find in many bakeries and shops throughout the town.

Peñaranda de Bracamonte

Another fascinating destination near Salamanca is Peñaranda de Bracamonte, a charming town located about 50 kilometers north of the city. Peñaranda is known for its medieval origins and beautiful plaza, as well as its old castles and noble palaces. The Palacio de los Duques de Alba, for example, is a stunning example of noble architecture, with its impressive stone façade and lush gardens.

The town is also home to the Iglesia de Nuestra Señora del Rosario, a beautiful church that reflects the area's rich architectural history. Peñaranda's local markets and traditional Spanish restaurants offer a taste of rural Castilla y León, with delicious local dishes and fresh produce.

Candelario

If you are looking to explore a traditional mountain village, head to Candelario, located in the Sierra de Béjar mountain range, about 80 kilometers from Salamanca. The village is known for its well-preserved traditional houses and wooden balconies. It's a great place to take a leisurely walk, with its narrow, winding streets offering a glimpse into village life in rural Spain.

Candelario is also famous for its fairs and festivals, particularly the Fiesta de la Vaca, where locals celebrate with music, dancing, and traditional rituals.

Adventure Activities and Nature Walks

Castilla y León's natural landscapes provide ample opportunities for adventure lovers to enjoy outdoor activities. Whether you're looking for scenic nature walks, adrenaline-pumping hikes, or peaceful cycling paths, this region is ideal for anyone who enjoys the great outdoors.

Hiking in the Sierra de Béjar

The Sierra de Béjar mountain range, located about 100 kilometers south of Salamanca, is home to some of the most scenic hiking trails in the region. The Cascada de las Noas (Waterfall of Noas) is a particularly stunning hike, where visitors can follow the trail through the lush forests and rocky outcrops to reach a beautiful waterfall. The Sierra de Béjar also offers great trails for cycling, with scenic routes weaving through picturesque valleys and mountain passes.

Arribes del Duero Natural Park

For those interested in more rugged terrain, the Arribes del Duero Natural Park, located about 80 kilometers west of Salamanca, offers dramatic gorges, rocky cliffs, and breathtaking riverscapes. It's an excellent destination for kayaking, rafting, or hiking. The park is also home to a rich diversity of wildlife, including eagles, vultures, and wild boar, making it a fantastic spot for birdwatching and nature photography.

If you're interested in a more relaxed exploration of the area, the Douro River, which runs through the park, is perfect for scenic boat tours. These tours provide a peaceful way to take in the natural beauty of the area while learning about the region's geography and flora.

The Historical City of Ávila

As mentioned earlier, Ávila is an absolute must-visit for history enthusiasts. Located just under two hours from Salamanca, this medieval city is one of Spain's best-preserved historical gems. Known primarily for its incredible medieval walls, which encircle the entire old town, Ávila is a UNESCO World Heritage site and offers a fascinating glimpse into Spain's past.

Medieval Walls of Ávila

The Ávila walls are the city's most prominent feature, stretching for more than 2.5 kilometers. These impressive fortifications date back to the 11th century and are made up of nearly 90 towers and 9 gates. Visitors can walk along the walls, experiencing the city's medieval atmosphere and taking in panoramic views of the surrounding countryside.

Monastery of San José

Another important landmark in Ávila is the Monastery of San José, founded by Saint Teresa of Ávila in the 16th century. The monastery is not only an architectural beauty but also a center of spiritual significance for those who follow the teachings of Saint Teresa. The monastery is a peaceful place to visit, offering a sense of serenity and spiritual reflection.

Visiting the Wine Regions of Castilla y León

Castilla y León is renowned for its exceptional wine regions, producing some of Spain's most celebrated wines. A visit to the nearby wine regions of Ribera del Duero, Rueda, and Toro offers an exciting opportunity to explore vineyards, taste wines, and learn about the region's deep-rooted winemaking traditions.

Ribera del Duero

Located to the north of Salamanca, Ribera del Duero is one of Spain's most prestigious wine regions, known for its rich, full-bodied red wines made from the Tempranillo grape. The region is home to many award-winning wineries, offering tours that allow visitors to explore the vineyards and cellars while tasting a variety of wines.

Bodegas Protos, located in the heart of the Ribera del Duero, is a famous winery where visitors can learn about the winemaking process and enjoy tastings of some of the region's finest wines. The region's beautiful vineyards, nestled along the Douro River, offer stunning scenery, making a visit to Ribera del Duero an unforgettable experience.

Rueda

Known for its white wines, particularly those made from the Verdejo grape, Rueda is another renowned wine region located to the east of Salamanca. The wines from Rueda are crisp and refreshing, making them perfect for pairing with Spanish seafood and cheese. Visitors can tour the region's wineries, learn about the winemaking process, and sample the wines in picturesque vineyard settings.

Bodegas Naia, located in the heart of Rueda, offers tours and tastings that provide an in-depth look into the art of winemaking in this famous region.

Toro

The Toro wine region, located further to the northwest of Salamanca, is famous for its bold red wines made from the Tinta de Toro grape. This region's rich soils and climate create wines that are powerful and intense, with deep flavors and complex aromas. Bodegas Fariña, one of the most prestigious wineries in the region, offers tours and tastings that allow visitors to explore Toro's winemaking heritage.

Salamanca is not just a city of history and culture; it is also a gateway to exploring the surrounding natural beauty, charming towns, and exceptional wine regions of Castilla y León. From outdoor adventures in the mountains to the rich cultural experiences in Ávila and the wine regions, there is something for every type of traveler. These day trips provide the perfect opportunity to experience the diverse landscapes, rich heritage, and vibrant culture that define this part of Spain. Whether you're an adventure seeker, a history buff, or a wine enthusiast, Salamanca and its surroundings offer a wealth of experiences that will stay with you long after your visit.

Chapter 10: Salamanca's Nightlife

Salamanca is a city that thrives after dark. Known for its lively student population, historic charm, and vibrant cultural scene, the city's nightlife offers something for everyone—from casual drinks in historic taverns to vibrant late-night clubs and cultural events. Whether you're a night owl seeking a relaxed evening at a wine bar, an adventurer looking for a high-energy club, or someone interested in immersing themselves in local music and traditions, Salamanca provides a diverse and exciting nightlife landscape. In this chapter, we explore the best bars, nightclubs, cultural events, and wine bars, showcasing the unique nighttime experiences that Salamanca offers.

Best Bars and Pubs

Salamanca's bar scene is a perfect mix of the traditional and the modern. The city is dotted with charming bars and pubs where locals and visitors come together to enjoy a drink, socialise, and unwind. Whether you prefer a cozy tavern with a traditional Spanish vibe or a modern bar with creative cocktails, Salamanca has it all.

Casa de las Conchas

A beloved spot in the heart of Salamanca, Casa de las Conchas is a historic bar located near the Casa de las Conchas (House of Shells), an iconic building in the city. This place, which is a mix of a historical landmark and a modern bar, offers a great place to grab a drink while admiring the beautiful stone walls adorned with seashells. The bar serves an impressive selection of local wines and spirits, as well as cocktails and tapas, making it a fantastic place for those looking for a bit of local charm.

La Chupitería

If you're in the mood for something a bit different, La Chupitería is a quirky, fun bar that specializes in shots. This lively spot is perfect for those looking to explore unique flavors and challenge their taste buds with a wide variety of shots, each with its own name and flavor profile. The décor is casual and fun, creating an energetic and playful atmosphere, which is ideal for a night of laughter and new experiences.

El Savor Café Bar

For a more relaxed and sophisticated environment, El Savor Café Bar offers an inviting atmosphere perfect for sipping cocktails or enjoying a glass of wine. Located in the city center, it has a cozy vibe, with a beautiful interior decorated in warm tones. The bar's cocktail list is diverse, offering both traditional and creative options. Whether you want to enjoy a classic gin and tonic or try something new, El Savor is a great choice for a laid-back evening.

Bambu Salamanca

Located close to the Plaza Mayor, Bambu Salamanca is a popular cocktail bar with an exotic flair. The bar serves expertly crafted cocktails using top-quality ingredients and offers a vibrant setting that attracts both locals and tourists. The large variety of cocktail options makes this a fun stop for those looking to unwind in a more contemporary, upbeat setting. Whether you're in the mood for a refreshing mojito or a spicy margarita, Bambu Salamanca has something for every taste.

Nightclubs and Late-Night Venues

Salamanca's nightlife wouldn't be complete without its thriving nightclubs and late-night venues, which cater to a range of musical tastes and atmospheres. Whether you're into dance music, hip-hop, or electronic beats, Salamanca has the perfect venue to keep you dancing until dawn.

Camelot Club

One of the top nightclubs in Salamanca, Camelot Club is a massive venue that draws crowds looking for an energetic and lively night out. Known for its electronic dance music (EDM) and commercial hits, Camelot attracts both locals and visitors from all over Spain. The club features a state-of-the-art sound system, impressive lighting, and a massive dance floor where you can groove all night. The atmosphere is electric, with DJs spinning the latest tracks, making it a popular choice for those looking to experience the city's vibrant nightlife scene.

Gabbana Salamanca

For those who enjoy a more upscale and glamorous nightlife experience, Gabbana Salamanca offers an exclusive clubbing experience. Located near the University of Salamanca, this nightclub is known for its luxurious interior, sophisticated ambiance, and top-notch service. Expect to hear a mix of commercial pop and Latin hits, and be prepared to enjoy a night of dancing in style. The venue also has a VIP section for those who want to enjoy a more private experience.

La Ventilla

For a more intimate late-night hangout, La Ventilla is a cozy club that has a warm, laid-back atmosphere. Known for its chilled vibes, this venue is a favorite among those who prefer more eclectic music such as indie rock, retro hits, and alternative music. The club's intimate size creates a more personal and cozy setting where guests can enjoy drinks, conversation, and dancing without the large crowds typically seen at other nightclubs.

Jazz Club Salamanca

For those who prefer live music and a more laid-back, jazz-filled experience, Jazz Club Salamanca offers a sophisticated and intimate space. Located in the city center, this venue hosts regular jazz performances, ranging from local talent to international musicians. The atmosphere is relaxed and welcoming, perfect for enjoying a cocktail while soaking in the smooth melodies of live jazz. The club is also known for its themed nights, which might include blues, soul, or Latin jazz, providing a diverse and immersive live music experience.

Music and Cultural Events

Salamanca is a city of culture, and its music and cultural events reflect the city's artistic heritage. From classical music to flamenco, there's something for everyone when it comes to live performances and cultural experiences in the evening.

Theater and Concerts at the Teatro Liceo

For those interested in a more refined and cultural experience, the Teatro Liceo offers an exciting range of performances throughout the year, including operas, classical music concerts, and theater productions. Located in a grand building that exudes old-world charm, this venue offers a perfect way to spend a more elegant evening in Salamanca. The programming at Teatro Liceo is diverse, with performances ranging from classical symphonies to more modern productions, catering to a wide array of tastes.

Flamenco Nights at Casa de la Guitarra

One of the highlights of Salamanca's cultural nightlife scene is its flamenco performances. Flamenco, the passionate and intense Spanish dance and music form, is an essential part of Spanish culture, and Casa de la Guitarra provides an authentic and intimate experience for those wanting to witness this spectacular art form. The venue is small, allowing for a personal connection to the performance, where skilled dancers and musicians bring flamenco to life through clapping, singing, and guitar playing. A night of flamenco at Casa de la Guitarra is a unique way to experience the soul of Spanish culture.

Festival Internacional de Jazz

If you're in Salamanca during the summer, you're in for a treat with the Festival Internacional de Jazz. Held annually, the jazz festival brings world-renowned jazz artists to the city for a series of open-air concerts, workshops, and jam sessions. Whether you're a jazz enthusiast or a casual listener, the festival offers a fantastic opportunity to experience top-tier performances in the beautiful setting of Plaza Mayor and other open-air venues. The festival is an essential part of Salamanca's cultural calendar, providing a world-class musical experience that everyone can enjoy.

Wine Bars and Flamenco Nights

Salamanca's vibrant nightlife also includes a growing selection of wine bars and flamenco nights, where guests can experience the city's gastronomy, traditional Spanish culture, and live performances in a relaxed setting. Whether you're a wine connoisseur or simply looking to unwind with a glass of local wine, Salamanca offers an array of venues to enjoy fine wines and intimate flamenco performances.

Bodegas El Conde

For wine lovers, Bodegas El Conde is one of the top spots to enjoy a selection of local wines from the surrounding Castilla y León region. Located in the Old Town, this wine bar offers a cozy, rustic atmosphere that invites guests to unwind and savor local wines such as Ribera del Duero and Rueda. The staff are knowledgeable and passionate about wine, offering expert recommendations to pair with their selection of delicious tapas.

The ambiance at Bodegas El Conde is relaxed, with low lighting and wooden furniture that evokes the traditional Spanish tavern. It's the ideal place for a quiet evening, whether you're a seasoned wine enthusiast or someone simply looking to enjoy a good glass in good company.

El Corral de la Pacheca

If you're looking for an authentic flamenco night in Salamanca, El Corral de la Pacheca offers one of the best experiences. This intimate venue hosts regular flamenco performances, showcasing the passion and artistry of traditional Spanish dance and music. As the music fills the air and the dancers' rhythmic movements take center stage, guests are transported to the heart of Andalusia. El Corral de la Pacheca also serves local tapas and wines, making it the perfect spot for an evening of authentic Spanish culture.

La Taberna del Loco

For a fun and lively night, La Taberna del Loco offers an exciting mix of live music and a laid-back bar atmosphere. Located in the heart of the city, this tavern is known for its casual vibe, energetic performances, and lively crowd. From flamenco to folk music, La Taberna del Loco regularly hosts performances that highlight Spain's rich musical traditions. Guests can enjoy tasty cocktails and local wines while tapping their feet to the rhythm of the music.

Salamanca's nightlife is an eclectic mix of tradition, culture, and modernity. Whether you're looking to enjoy a quiet glass of wine in a cozy bar, dance the night away in a lively nightclub, immerse yourself in a passionate flamenco performance, or experience world-class jazz concerts, Salamanca offers something for every type of night owl.

Chapter 11: Cultural Experiences in Salamanca

Salamanca is a city that seamlessly blends its rich historical legacy with a vibrant cultural scene. Known for its renowned university, medieval architecture, and picturesque streets, the city is a cultural gem in the heart of Spain. From its impressive museums and art galleries to lively flamenco performances and traditional festivals, Salamanca offers a wealth of experiences that celebrate its diverse artistic, musical, and cultural traditions. This chapter takes you through the best cultural experiences in Salamanca, providing an in-depth exploration of its museums, flamenco and traditional dance shows, local festivals, Spanish music and opera, and the art of pottery that has been perfected in the region for centuries.

Museums and Art Galleries

Salamanca is home to an impressive collection of museums and art galleries that showcase the city's rich artistic and intellectual history. Whether you're an art lover, a history enthusiast, or someone curious about the region's cultural development, these institutions provide a fascinating insight into the heritage of this historic city.

Museo de Art Nouveau y Art Déco (Museum of Art Nouveau and Art Deco)

One of the hidden gems of Salamanca, the Museo de Art Nouveau y Art Déco is dedicated to the artistic movements of the late 19th and early 20th centuries. Housed in the Palacio de Figueroa, a beautiful Renaissance-style palace, this museum boasts a remarkable collection of Art Nouveau and Art Deco pieces, including furniture, glass, ceramics, and sculptures. Visitors can admire works by prominent artists from these movements, offering a stunning contrast to the historical architecture of the city. This museum is an ideal place for those who appreciate modernist design and wish to learn more about the decorative arts of the period.

Museo de la Historia de la Automoción (Museum of the History of Automobiles)

A unique and fascinating museum in Salamanca, the Museo de la Historia de la Automoción takes visitors on a journey through the history of cars, from their early models to more contemporary designs. The museum showcases an extensive collection of classic cars, motorcycles, and automobile-related memorabilia. The collection also highlights the evolution of car manufacturing techniques and the impact of the automobile on Spanish society. This museum provides a different perspective on history and technology, making it an excellent stop for those interested in cars and industrial design.

Museo de Salamanca (Salamanca Museum)

For a deeper look into the city's history and culture, the Museo de Salamanca is a must-visit. Located in a former convent, the museum spans several floors and houses exhibits on the region's prehistoric past, Roman and medieval history, as well as its Renaissance and Baroque art. One of the museum's standout collections is its Roman artifacts, which include sculptures, mosaics, and everyday objects from the Roman settlement of Helmantica (ancient Salamanca). The museum also hosts temporary exhibitions and educational programs, making it an engaging destination for visitors of all ages.

Centro de Arte Contemporáneo (Center for Contemporary Art)

For those interested in contemporary art, the Centro de Arte Contemporáneo is the place to go. Housed in a modernist building, this art center features rotating exhibitions of contemporary artists, focusing on Spanish and international avant-garde art. The center's programming includes painting, sculpture, photography, and multimedia installations, offering visitors a chance to engage with cutting-edge artistic practices. The space itself is a work of art, designed to foster interaction between the viewer and the artwork, creating an immersive cultural experience.

Flamenco and Traditional Dance Shows

Flamenco is an integral part of Spain's cultural heritage, and Salamanca offers a variety of opportunities to experience this passionate and powerful art form. Whether in intimate taverns or larger theaters, the rhythmic claps, soulful guitar playing, and intense footwork of flamenco dancers offer a dynamic glimpse into Spain's vibrant cultural traditions.

Casa de la Guitarra

For an authentic and intimate flamenco experience, Casa de la Guitarra is a must-see venue in Salamanca. This intimate cultural space hosts regular flamenco shows, featuring talented dancers, singers, and guitarists. The cozy setting allows for an up-close and personal connection with the performers, creating an immersive experience that transports visitors to the heart of Andalusia. The performances are typically intense and passionate, showcasing the full range of flamenco's emotional expression. With a glass of Sherry or local wine in hand, Casa de la Guitarra offers an unforgettable evening of flamenco.

El Corral de la Pacheca

Another excellent venue for experiencing flamenco is El Corral de la Pacheca, a traditional tavern dedicated to flamenco performances. Located near the Plaza Mayor, this venue offers an authentic and lively atmosphere where visitors can enjoy a mix of flamenco and Spanish folk music. The intimate setting, combined with talented artists, provides an unforgettable night out. El Corral de la Pacheca also serves traditional tapas and drinks, allowing guests to enjoy an immersive Spanish experience while watching captivating flamenco performances.

Teatro Liceo

For those looking to experience flamenco on a larger scale, Teatro Liceo hosts annual flamenco festivals and special performances by renowned flamenco companies. The theater's grand interior adds an extra layer of sophistication to the flamenco experience, as audiences enjoy the music and dance in an elegant setting. The performances here are known for their professionalism and their dedication to preserving traditional flamenco while also introducing contemporary elements to the art form.

Local Festivals and Celebrations

Salamanca is known for its lively festivals and celebrations that showcase the city's traditions, religious practices, and cultural heritage. From its medieval festivals to lively annual events, Salamanca's calendar is filled with festivals that attract visitors from all over the world. Experiencing these celebrations is a fantastic way to immerse yourself in the city's cultural life.

Fiesta de la Virgen de la Vega

One of the most important festivals in Salamanca is the Fiesta de la Virgen de la Vega, which takes place in early September. This religious and cultural event honors the Virgen de la Vega, the patron saint of Salamanca. The festival is marked by religious processions, live music, fireworks, and a colorful parade. During the festivities, the streets are filled with locals dressed in traditional Castilian costumes, and the city comes alive with cultural performances and dancing. The Plaza Mayor is the focal point of the festival, hosting events throughout the day and night, making it an excellent time to visit Salamanca.

Semana Santa (Holy Week)

Salamanca's Semana Santa (Holy Week) is a deeply religious and cultural celebration that draws both locals and visitors. The processions that take place throughout the week are some of the most beautiful and significant in Spain, with participants carrying religious statues and iconography through the streets of the old town. The procession on Good Friday, in particular, is the highlight of the week, with thousands of people gathering to witness the solemn and dramatic displays of faith. The celebration is an extraordinary mix of religion, art, and culture, making it one of the most memorable events in Salamanca.

Festival Internacional de las Artes de Castilla y León (FACYL)

The Festival Internacional de las Artes de Castilla y León is an annual cultural festival that takes place in Salamanca and throughout the region. It brings together artists, performers, and musicians from around the world for a celebration of creativity and cultural exchange. The festival features a wide range of performances, including theater, dance, music, and visual arts. FACYL provides a platform for both established and emerging artists, and it is an excellent event for those looking to experience the artistic diversity of Salamanca.

Traditional Spanish Music and Opera

Salamanca's cultural scene is also rich in traditional Spanish music and opera. With a variety of venues dedicated to the performing arts, the city offers a range of opportunities to enjoy live classical and contemporary music, from intimate performances to grand opera productions.

Teatro Liceo (Opera)

For those who enjoy opera, Teatro Liceo is one of Salamanca's premier venues. Known for its beautiful interior and excellent acoustics, the theater hosts regular opera performances, often featuring famous works by composers like Verdi, Puccini, and Mozart. In addition to opera, the theater also hosts ballet and classical music concerts, making it a hub for those interested in high culture and performing arts.

Conciertos de la Universidad de Salamanca

As home to one of Europe's oldest universities, Salamanca also offers a rich tradition of academic musical performances. The Conciertos de la Universidad de Salamanca feature a series of classical music concerts that showcase the talents of student musicians and visiting performers. These concerts often take place in the historic Auditorio de la Universidad, offering visitors a chance to enjoy exceptional music in an intimate, scholarly environment.

La Sede de la Música

For fans of traditional Spanish music, La Sede de la Música is a must-visit venue. It offers a range of performances, from flamenco to classical guitar recitals. The venue prides itself on promoting Spanish music traditions, and many of its performances showcase the best of Spanish classical and folk music. If you want to experience Spain's deep musical heritage, this is the place to go.

The Art of Spanish Pottery in Salamanca

One of Salamanca's hidden treasures is its pottery and ceramics, which have been an important part of the region's cultural heritage for centuries. Salamanca has a long tradition of producing handcrafted pottery, known for its quality, craftsmanship, and unique designs. The city's artisans still create traditional ceramics that reflect the style and techniques of earlier generations.

Cerámica Salmantina

Cerámica Salmantina is a family-owned workshop and store where visitors can learn about the intricate process of making traditional Salamanca ceramics. The workshop produces a range of products, from decorative plates and vases to functional items such as mugs and bowls. The pieces are often decorated with colorful geometric patterns, floral motifs, and local symbols, making them perfect souvenirs of your visit. Visitors can tour the workshop, watch the artisans at work, and even purchase handmade ceramics to take home.

Alfarería de La Abuela

For an authentic pottery experience, Alfarería de La Abuela offers a glimpse into the traditional art of pottery-making in Salamanca. This workshop specializes in hand-thrown pottery, using techniques that have been passed down through generations. The shop is a charming place to explore the art of Spanish ceramics, and the friendly artisans are happy to explain the processes involved in creating each piece. Whether you're looking for a unique gift or simply wish to appreciate the skill involved in making these beautiful ceramics, Alfarería de La Abuela offers an enriching experience.

Salamanca is a city that celebrates culture in every corner, from its museums and galleries to its flamenco performances and local festivals. The city's cultural life reflects its deep history and artistic traditions, offering visitors an array of enriching experiences that showcase both its past and present. Whether you're strolling through its museums, enjoying a live performance, or witnessing a traditional festival, Salamanca invites you to immerse yourself in its rich cultural tapestry.

Chapter 12: Outdoor Activities and Parks

Salamanca is a city that celebrates the outdoors, offering visitors a wealth of natural spaces, outdoor activities, and recreational areas. Whether you're looking to relax in one of the city's beautiful parks, embark on an active adventure with cycling and hiking, enjoy water activities on the River Tormes, or explore the stunning surrounding mountains, Salamanca provides a perfect blend of nature, adventure, and tranquility. This chapter takes you through the best outdoor activities and parks in Salamanca, providing you with the ultimate guide to enjoying the city's green spaces and natural beauty.

Parks and Green Spaces

Salamanca is home to a variety of parks and green spaces that provide the perfect environment for relaxation, family outings, or simply enjoying the natural beauty of the city. These parks offer an oasis of calm amidst the city's historic streets, making them ideal spots for those seeking respite from the bustle of daily life.

Parque de los Jesuitas

One of the largest and most popular parks in Salamanca is the Parque de los Jesuitas. Located near the University of Salamanca, this park offers vast green lawns, shaded areas, and beautiful walking paths. With its tranquil atmosphere, Parque de los Jesuitas is a favorite among locals and visitors alike for a relaxing stroll, a family picnic, or even a casual jog. The park is dotted with trees that provide ample shade, making it a popular place for students, families, and tourists to unwind.

The park also features well-maintained playgrounds, making it an excellent destination for families with children. The large grassy areas are perfect for sports activities, and you can often find locals playing football or enjoying a friendly game of catch. If you're visiting during the summer, you may even come across open-air concerts or cultural events held in the park.

Parque de la Alamedilla

Situated just outside the city center, Parque de la Alamedilla is another beautiful green space in Salamanca. It is one of the oldest parks in the city, offering visitors a mix of wide-open spaces and peaceful corners to enjoy. The park is ideal for walking, running, or simply relaxing with a book while surrounded by nature. With its ponds, flower beds, and trees, Parque de la Alamedilla is a calming retreat for anyone seeking a break from the urban environment.

The park also has a fountain that is popular for photography and a cafeteria, where visitors can grab a coffee or a refreshing drink. Parque de la Alamedilla is known for being well-maintained, offering a comfortable and inviting atmosphere throughout the year.

Parque de la Vaguada

Located on the outskirts of Salamanca, Parque de la Vaguada is a lesser-known but equally beautiful park that offers a peaceful escape. The park is home to a variety of flora and fauna, making it a wonderful spot for nature lovers. The walking paths wind through the park, and the large lakes are home to ducks, geese, and other birds. Parque de la Vaguada is a great destination for those who enjoy birdwatching or simply want to enjoy a quieter park that is away from the crowds.

The park's open-air spaces are perfect for sports or leisure activities, and it also has picnic areas where visitors can enjoy meals with family and friends. Whether you're looking to take a walk, have a picnic, or simply relax in a green space, Parque de la Vaguada is a lovely place to visit.

Cycling and Hiking Trails

Salamanca and its surrounding areas offer a variety of cycling and hiking trails that cater to outdoor enthusiasts of all levels. With its beautiful landscapes, rolling hills, and scenic countryside, the region provides ample opportunities for adventure, whether you prefer to explore by foot or by bike.

Cycling in and around Salamanca

Salamanca is a relatively bike-friendly city, with several dedicated cycling lanes and paths for cyclists to explore. Calle de Toro, one of the city's main shopping streets, is a great starting point for cycling tours through the city, offering scenic views of the historic buildings as you make your way through the streets. For those looking for more adventure, there are numerous cycling routes around Salamanca that take you out into the countryside.

One popular route is the Vía Verde de la Plata, which runs through the countryside to the south of Salamanca. This greenway follows an old railway line and is ideal for cyclists who want to enjoy rural landscapes, rolling hills, and beautiful views. The trail is well-maintained, and cyclists can enjoy a peaceful ride through the Sierra de Francia mountain range, passing through small villages, forests, and open fields. It's a perfect way to enjoy the region's natural beauty while getting some exercise.

Hiking Trails in Salamanca

For hiking enthusiasts, Salamanca offers a range of trails that take you through both urban areas and rural landscapes. The Sierra de Béjar mountains, located to the south of the city, provide some of the most spectacular hiking routes. The Cascada de las Noas hike, for instance, is a moderately challenging trail that leads to a beautiful waterfall. The hike offers stunning views of the surrounding hills, with the trail passing through forests and along streams.

Another great hiking option is the Arribes del Duero Natural Park, located about 80 kilometers from Salamanca. The park offers numerous hiking trails that wind through the gorges, rivers, and hills of this unique natural area. The Cañones del Duero trail, for example, takes hikers along the edge of the Douro River and offers breathtaking views of the cliffs and ravines that characterize the landscape. Hikers can also enjoy birdwatching along the trail, as the park is home to a variety of wildlife, including vultures, eagles, and deer.

Rutas de Senderismo de la Sierra de Francia

The Sierra de Francia mountains are a popular destination for those seeking more challenging hiking routes. With its rocky paths, dense forests, and picturesque villages, the area is perfect for those who want to experience the more rugged side of Salamanca's countryside. The Ruta de las 5 Villas, a circular route that passes through several mountain villages, is one of the best ways to explore this area. The route includes a mixture of easy and moderate hikes, and hikers are treated to views of the river valleys and mountain ranges that define the region.

River Tormes and Water Activities

The River Tormes runs through the heart of Salamanca, offering a variety of water-based activities for those who want to explore the city from a different perspective. The river is an important natural feature of the city, and several parks and green spaces are located along its banks, making it the perfect spot for a relaxing day by the water. For more adventurous types, the river also offers a range of water activities.

Kayaking and Canoeing

One of the best ways to experience the River Tormes is by kayaking or canoeing. The river is calm and ideal for beginners, offering a relaxing experience as you paddle along its course, surrounded by beautiful natural scenery. Kayaking along the river gives you the chance to see the city's historic bridges, such as the Roman Bridge, from a unique perspective.

Several companies in Salamanca offer kayak and canoe rentals, and guided tours are available for those who want to explore the river with an expert guide. Whether you're a seasoned kayaker or a beginner, paddling along the River Tormes is an unforgettable experience.

Riverfront Walks and Cycling

If you prefer to stay dry, the riverfront promenades along the River Tormes offer beautiful scenic walking and cycling paths. The Paseo de los Olivos is a popular path that runs alongside the river, offering breathtaking views of the water and the surrounding natural landscape. It's a great place for a leisurely stroll or a relaxing bike ride, and it's perfect for those who want to enjoy the outdoors without venturing too far from the city center.

The Puente Romano, the Roman Bridge that spans the river, provides an excellent spot to stop and admire the view of the water. The riverbanks are lined with parks and gardens, making it a peaceful and scenic place to spend the day.

Fishing

For those who enjoy fishing, the River Tormes offers opportunities for both freshwater and fly fishing. The river is home to various species of fish, including barbel, trout, and carp, making it a popular spot for anglers. Fishing permits are available for those who want to enjoy a peaceful day by the water, either on the riverbanks or from a boat.

Exploring the Surrounding Mountains

The region surrounding Salamanca is home to stunning mountain ranges, providing ample opportunities for outdoor exploration. Whether you're looking for a challenging hike or a more relaxing nature walk, the mountains of Castilla y León offer breathtaking views and diverse landscapes to discover.

Sierra de Béjar

One of the most popular mountainous areas near Salamanca is the Sierra de Béjar, located south of the city. The range is known for its rugged terrain, steep cliffs, and dense forests. This mountain range is a haven for hikers and outdoor enthusiasts, offering a variety of trails that cater to different levels of experience.

In addition to hiking, the Sierra de Béjar is a popular spot for skiing in the winter months, with the La Covatilla Ski Resort offering slopes for all skill levels. In the warmer months, the area transforms into a hiker's paradise, with trails that lead through oak forests and up to mountain summits, providing stunning panoramic views of the surrounding countryside.

Sierra de Francia

Another prominent mountain range near Salamanca is the Sierra de Francia, located to the south. This range is known for its rugged landscapes, charming villages, and historical significance. The Sierra de Francia is part of the Arribes del Duero Natural Park, which is known for its dramatic gorges and river valleys.

The area is perfect for those who enjoy challenging hikes, with routes that take you through mountain passes and along river canyons. Many of the trails lead to historic villages such as La Alberca and Mogarraz, where you can experience the region's traditional architecture and culture. The views from the mountain tops are absolutely spectacular, making it a must-see destination for those interested in both nature and history.

Salamanca offers a wealth of outdoor activities that allow visitors to immerse themselves in its natural beauty and explore the surrounding landscapes. From peaceful parks in the city to rugged mountain hikes, the region provides ample opportunities for outdoor exploration. Whether you're paddling down the River Tormes, cycling through rural landscapes, or hiking the majestic Sierra de Béjar, Salamanca has something for everyone. Its combination of green spaces, water activities, and mountainous terrain makes it the perfect destination for outdoor enthusiasts seeking a blend of adventure, tranquility, and natural beauty.

Chapter 13: Salamanca for Families

Salamanca is an ideal destination for families looking to enjoy a memorable vacation in a city rich with history, culture, and natural beauty. The city offers a wide range of family-friendly attractions, interactive activities, and dining options that cater to both parents and children. Whether you're exploring historic landmarks, enjoying outdoor spaces, or learning through hands-on experiences, Salamanca provides a welcoming environment for families to bond, learn, and have fun together. This chapter will guide you through the best kid-friendly attractions, family dining experiences, helpful tips for traveling with children, and interactive experiences that will keep young minds engaged and entertained throughout your visit.

Kid-Friendly Attractions and Activities

Salamanca is packed with a variety of attractions that are perfect for families, offering activities that are both fun and educational. From historical sites that bring the past to life to modern spaces that encourage creativity and play, Salamanca is a city that offers something for every age group.

Parque de los Jesuitas

One of the best parks for families in Salamanca is the Parque de los Jesuitas, a spacious and green area where children can run, play, and explore. This park is home to wide lawns, playgrounds, and walking paths, making it a great place to spend an afternoon with young children. The park is also equipped with benches, providing plenty of seating for parents to relax while the kids enjoy the fresh air. With its peaceful atmosphere and ample space, Parque de los Jesuitas is the perfect spot for a family picnic or casual outdoor games.

Additionally, the park is surrounded by historical buildings and landmarks, including the nearby University of Salamanca and Iglesia de San Esteban, making it a great spot to introduce children to the city's rich cultural history while enjoying outdoor activities.

Casa de las Conchas

The Casa de las Conchas, or House of Shells, is another family-friendly attraction in Salamanca. This beautiful 15th-century building is covered in over 300 sculpted shells, which kids will love to spot as they wander around the façade. The Casa de las Conchas is home to a public library, so families can explore the interior and enjoy the peaceful atmosphere inside. The staircase, which is adorned with intricate carvings and medieval motifs, is an excellent example of traditional Spanish architecture and provides a fun and educational experience for children interested in history and art.

Since the building is centrally located, families can easily add this stop to their sightseeing itinerary while exploring the city center.

Museo de Historia Natural (Natural History Museum)

The Museo de Historia Natural is a perfect place for children to learn about the natural world in an interactive and engaging way. Located near the Plaza Mayor, the museum features exhibits on various topics, including local wildlife, dinosaurs, and evolution. Kids can see fossils, animal skeletons, and interactive displays that make learning fun. The museum also offers educational programs and activities designed to engage children, making it an excellent stop for families who want to combine fun and learning.

The museum's approachable and educational exhibits provide a great introduction to science for young visitors, sparking curiosity and encouraging questions about the natural world.

La Rana de Salamanca (The Frog of Salamanca)

A fun and quirky tradition in Salamanca is the search for the frog hidden on the façade of the Escuelas Mayores (the main building of the University of Salamanca). According to legend, if you spot the frog, you'll enjoy good luck during your time in the city. This activity is a fun game for children, and it also offers a great way for families to engage with the historical and architectural significance of the University of Salamanca. The frog is cleverly hidden among the intricate carvings on the building's façade, providing an enjoyable challenge for kids as they try to find it.

While searching for the frog, families can also take in the grandeur of the Plaza Mayor and explore the other nearby landmarks.

Aquarium of Salamanca

Located a short drive outside the city center, the Aquarium of Salamanca is a fantastic family attraction. The aquarium is home to a variety of marine life from around the world, including sharks, sea turtles, and tropical fish. The aquarium offers children a chance to learn about ocean conservation and the importance of protecting marine ecosystems. The interactive exhibits are designed to engage young visitors, making it both an entertaining and educational outing.

Families can enjoy exploring the various themed sections, such as the Amazon Rainforest and the Mediterranean Sea, as well as watching feeding demonstrations and participating in hands-on activities.

Family Dining and Entertainment

Salamanca boasts a vibrant dining scene with plenty of family-friendly restaurants and entertainment options that cater to young tastes and preferences. Whether you're looking for a casual spot to enjoy traditional Spanish cuisine or a themed restaurant that will entertain your little ones, Salamanca offers a variety of options that make dining out with kids a fun experience.

La Vaca y La Huerta

A great family-friendly restaurant in Salamanca is La Vaca y La Huerta, which serves delicious, locally sourced farm-to-table food. The restaurant has a warm and welcoming atmosphere, with a casual vibe that's perfect for families. The menu offers a variety of kid-friendly options, including traditional Spanish dishes like croquetas, paella, and grilled meats, all made with fresh, seasonal ingredients. For children with specific dietary preferences, La Vaca y La Huerta also offers vegetarian and gluten-free options, ensuring that everyone in the family is well-catered for.

The restaurant also features a play area where children can enjoy games and activities while waiting for their meal, making it a great option for families with young children.

Bamboo Salamanca

For a more relaxed dining experience, Bamboo Salamanca is a cozy restaurant that offers a wide selection of food, from pasta and burgers to tapas and grilled dishes. It is particularly well-suited for families, as it offers both indoor and outdoor seating in a relaxed, modern environment. The kid-friendly menu includes favorites such as pasta, chicken nuggets, and fresh fruit, making it a great place for younger children to enjoy a meal. With its casual atmosphere and delicious food, Bamboo Salamanca is perfect for a family night out.

Themed Restaurants and Entertainment

For families with young children, themed restaurants and entertainment spots provide a fun way to dine while enjoying a unique experience. While Salamanca doesn't have many exclusively themed restaurants, you can find some spots where children's entertainment is included. La Taberna del Loco is one such venue where families can enjoy dinner while watching live performances, including musicians, comedians, and even magic shows. The relaxed environment and entertaining performances ensure that children are entertained while parents can enjoy a delicious meal.

Tips for Traveling with Children

Traveling with children can be an exciting experience, but it also requires some planning and preparation. To ensure a smooth and enjoyable visit to Salamanca with your family, here are some practical tips to help you make the most of your trip.

Pack Smart and Be Prepared

When traveling to Salamanca, especially with younger children, it's important to pack for all types of weather. While the city enjoys warm summers, the evenings can get chilly, especially in the spring and fall. Packing layers and a light jacket will help ensure that everyone stays comfortable. Also, make sure to bring snacks and water bottles for long days of sightseeing, as there are plenty of opportunities to rest and enjoy a snack in the city's beautiful parks and cafes.

Take Advantage of Public Transportation

Salamanca has an efficient and family-friendly public transportation system. The city's bus network covers most of the key attractions, and the buses are clean, safe, and easy to use. If you're traveling with a stroller, the buses are accessible, and children often travel at a reduced fare. Using public transportation is a great way to navigate the city with kids, allowing you to rest between attractions and avoid long walks in the heat.

Plan for Downtime

Traveling with children can be tiring, especially if you're trying to see everything in a short period. Be sure to schedule downtime in your itinerary, allowing time for your kids to relax and recharge. This could be as simple as a visit to a local park or a leisurely lunch at one of the family-friendly restaurants. Salamanca's parks, such as Parque de los Jesuitas and Parque de la Alamedilla, offer plenty of space for kids to run and play, ensuring that they stay energized throughout the day.

Look for Family Deals and Passes

Many of Salamanca's attractions offer family-friendly tickets or discounts for children. For example, museums such as the Museo de Historia Natural and Museo de Salamanca often provide free admission for children under a certain age. Be sure to check in advance for any special family passes or discounts, as these can help save money and make it easier to plan your visit.

Interactive and Educational Experiences for Kids

Salamanca is not only a city of culture and history but also one that offers plenty of opportunities for children to learn through interactive and hands-on experiences. These activities provide young minds with the chance to engage with the city's history, art, and science in a fun and educational way.

Museo de Historia Natural (Natural History Museum)

The Museo de Historia Natural offers one of the most engaging and educational experiences for children in Salamanca. The museum features a wide variety of exhibits, ranging from dinosaur fossils to local wildlife and geological formations. The museum includes interactive displays where children can learn about the environment, biodiversity, and the history of life on Earth. There are also touch-screen displays and educational games that make learning fun for kids of all ages.

Science and Educational Workshops

Salamanca also offers a number of educational workshops and hands-on activities aimed at children. Many of the city's museums and cultural centers, including the Museo de Salamanca and Centro de Arte Contemporáneo, host interactive workshops that allow children to engage with art and history. These workshops encourage creativity and learning through activities like painting, crafting, and science experiments. Check local listings to see if any workshops or special events are taking place during your visit.

Farm Visits and Animal Experiences

For families looking for a more rural experience, nearby farms and animal sanctuaries provide an excellent opportunity for children to learn about agriculture, animal care, and the environment. These visits often include interactive activities, such as feeding animals, helping with farm chores, and learning about traditional farming methods.

Salamanca is a fantastic destination for families, offering a variety of kid-friendly attractions, outdoor activities, and educational experiences. From parks and green spaces to museums and interactive workshops, the city provides a wide range of activities that both children and parents will enjoy. With its combination of history, culture, and nature, Salamanca offers a unique opportunity for families to spend quality time together while exploring all that this beautiful Spanish city has to offer. Whether you're hiking through the countryside, enjoying a meal at a family-friendly restaurant, or experiencing a flamenco performance, Salamanca is sure to create lasting memories for families of all ages.

Chapter 14: Salamanca's History and Architecture

Salamanca is a city steeped in history, where every street, building, and monument tells a story of past civilizations that have shaped its rich cultural identity. Known for its historical landmarks, stunning architecture, and intellectual legacy, Salamanca stands as one of Spain's most significant cities, attracting visitors from around the world who come to experience its blend of Roman, Moorish, Renaissance, and Baroque influences. This chapter will guide you through Salamanca's architectural evolution, with a focus on its Roman influences, the Moorish and Renaissance architecture, and some of its most important historical landmarks. We will also walk you through the medieval streets and explore the ancient walls and monuments that have made Salamanca a UNESCO World Heritage site.

Roman Influence on the City

Salamanca's history stretches back to ancient times, and its roots can be traced to the Roman period, which had a lasting influence on the city's architectural landscape. The Romans first established a settlement in the area in the 2nd century BCE, calling it

Helmantica. Although much of the Roman influence on Salamanca has been obscured by time, several key remnants of Roman life can still be seen throughout the city.

The Roman Bridge (Puente Romano)

The most prominent Roman landmark in Salamanca is the Roman Bridge (Puente Romano), which spans the River Tormes. Built in the 1st century CE, this bridge is a testament to the Romans' impressive engineering skills and ability to create structures that stood the test of time. The bridge originally had 26 arches and was an essential route for travelers crossing the river. Today, visitors can walk across the bridge and enjoy panoramic views of the riverbank and the historic city center.

The Roman Bridge is one of the few remaining examples of Roman engineering in Salamanca and serves as a reminder of the city's role as a vital Roman settlement. Its continued existence over two millennia speaks to the durability and ingenuity of Roman construction.

Roman Ruins and Archaeological Sites

Beneath the surface of modern Salamanca lies an extensive network of Roman ruins that offer insight into the city's ancient past. Archaeological excavations have revealed remnants of Roman buildings, roads, and forums that once formed the core of Helmantica. Some of these remains can be viewed at the Museo de Salamanca, which houses a collection of Roman artifacts, including mosaics, sculptures, and pottery.

The Calle del Teso de la Feria is another site where remnants of Roman baths have been uncovered, giving visitors a glimpse into the everyday life of the Roman citizens who once lived in the area. Although much of Roman Salamanca is buried beneath the city's modern infrastructure, these ruins remind us of the city's ancient heritage.

Moorish and Renaissance Architecture

After the fall of the Roman Empire, Salamanca was influenced by a series of different cultures, with Moorish and Renaissance architecture playing particularly significant roles in shaping the city's development. During the Middle Ages, the Moors left an indelible mark on Salamanca's architectural style, followed by the Renaissance period, which brought new ideas and grandeur to the city's structures.

Moorish Influence in Salamanca

The influence of the Moors, who occupied much of Spain from the 8th to the 15th centuries, can be seen in various parts of Salamanca. One of the most notable examples of Moorish architecture in the city is the Iglesia del Marqués de San Esteban, a church that retains elements of Islamic design, such as its horseshoe arches and intricate geometric patterns. These architectural features, typical of Islamic art, provide a visual link to the Moors' time in the Iberian Peninsula.

Additionally, the Casa de las Conchas (House of Shells), though more commonly associated with the Renaissance period, has been influenced by Moorish styles. The distinctive shell motifs that cover its façade are believed to have originated from Moorish architecture, and the building's courtyard also exhibits elements typical of Islamic design, such as its arcades and open spaces.

Renaissance Influence

Salamanca's Renaissance architecture reflects the city's growing prominence during the 16th century as a center of learning and culture. This period of architectural development was influenced by both Italian Renaissance ideals and Spain's own national identity.

One of the most prominent examples of Renaissance architecture in Salamanca is the University of Salamanca. Founded in 1134 and restructured during the Renaissance, the university's Escuelas Mayores (Main Building) features a stunning façade, with elements of Renaissance and Plateresque decoration. The Plateresque style, a Spanish variation of Renaissance architecture, is characterized by intricate detailing and ornamental motifs, which can be seen on the university's façade, including the famous frog carving.

The Palacio de Monterrey, another Renaissance masterpiece in Salamanca, features a majestic combination of classical design and Italian Renaissance influences. Built in the late 15th century, the palace served as a residence for Spanish nobility, with its symmetrical façade and grand courtyard highlighting the Renaissance ideals of balance and harmony.

Historical Landmarks and Sites

Salamanca is home to some of Spain's most important historical landmarks and sites, each representing a different chapter in the city's long and varied history. These landmarks not only offer visitors a window into the past but also reflect the city's artistic and cultural evolution over the centuries.

Plaza Mayor

One of the most iconic landmarks in Salamanca is the Plaza Mayor, the city's central square, which dates back to the 18th century. The Plaza Mayor is an example of Baroque architecture, with its grand stone arcades and balconies offering a sense of grandeur and openness. The square has served as a gathering place for locals and visitors alike for centuries and remains one of the most lively and vibrant spots in the city.

The Plaza Mayor is a hub of activity, hosting cultural events, festivals, and public celebrations. It is also surrounded by cafes and restaurants, making it an ideal spot to sit and watch the world go by. The plaza's architecture is a fine example of how Baroque styles merged with Spanish traditions, making it an important symbol of Salamanca's cultural significance.

Catedral Vieja and Catedral Nueva (Old and New Cathedrals)

Salamanca's Cathedrals are among the city's most impressive architectural and religious landmarks. The Catedral Vieja (Old Cathedral), built in the 12th century, is a stunning example of Romanesque architecture, with its imposing structure, elaborate carvings, and painted frescoes. The cathedral is home to the Pórtico de la Gloria, a monumental Romanesque portal, which is one of the finest examples of Romanesque sculpture in Spain.

In contrast, the Catedral Nueva (New Cathedral), built between the 16th and 18th centuries, exemplifies Gothic and Baroque styles. The New Cathedral's tall spires and ornate interior make it one of the most stunning cathedrals in Spain. The altarpiece and chapels are decorated with incredible works of art, and the cathedral's massive size allows visitors to fully appreciate its architectural splendor.

Convento de San Esteban

The Convento de San Esteban (Convent of Saint Stephen) is another notable historical landmark in Salamanca, particularly for those interested in religious history. Founded in the 16th century, the convent is a beautiful example of Spanish Baroque architecture. The facade of the convent is intricately detailed, with stone carvings and religious motifs that reflect the Counter-Reformation ideals of the time.

The convent's church features an impressive altar and ceiling covered in painted frescoes, depicting scenes from the life of Saint Stephen. Visitors can also explore the monastic rooms and cloisters, offering a sense of peace and contemplation.

Walking Through Salamanca's Medieval Streets

One of the most enjoyable ways to experience Salamanca's architectural beauty is by wandering through its medieval streets. These historic pathways offer a glimpse into the city's past, with narrow alleys, ancient stone buildings, and well-preserved structures that have remained largely unchanged for centuries.

Calle Mayor and Calle de la Rúa

Calle Mayor and Calle de la Rúa are two of the most iconic medieval streets in Salamanca, leading visitors through the heart of the city. These pedestrian streets are lined with historic buildings, including Renaissance and Baroque facades, giving them a distinct charm that reflects the city's architectural evolution. As you walk along these streets, you'll pass through centuries-old archways and see local artisans selling their wares, providing a unique opportunity to experience Salamanca's medieval atmosphere.

Calle de San Pablo

Another charming medieval street is Calle de San Pablo, located near the University of Salamanca. This street is home to several historic buildings and monuments, including the Iglesia de San Pablo, a beautiful Gothic church with an ornate façade. As you walk down this street, you'll encounter stone buildings with decorative facades and narrow alleyways, creating a sense of stepping back in time to the city's medieval past.

Walking through these medieval streets is an immersive experience that allows you to appreciate Salamanca's rich history and architecture at your own pace, while also discovering hidden gems along the way.

Ancient Walls and Monuments

Salamanca is home to several ancient walls and monuments that tell the story of the city's strategic importance throughout history. These fortifications and monuments are not only architectural marvels but also key elements in understanding the city's defense and cultural heritage.

Murallas de Salamanca (City Walls)

The Murallas de Salamanca (City Walls) are one of the most impressive historical landmarks in the city. These medieval walls were built to protect the city from invaders during the Middle Ages. Although much of the original structure has been altered or destroyed over time, portions of the walls still stand today, particularly near the Puente Romano and the Iglesia de San Juan de Sahagún. The city gates, such as Puerta de la Ciudad and Puerta de San Martín, are also remnants of the original walls and offer insight into the city's fortifications during the medieval period.

Monumento a Franco and Plaza de la Concordia

One of Salamanca's prominent monuments is the Monumento a Franco, located in Plaza de la Concordia. Although controversial due to its association with the Spanish Civil War and Francisco Franco's dictatorship, this monument reflects the complex history of Salamanca. The statue is part of the city's effort to preserve historical monuments from different periods, offering visitors a chance to learn about Spain's political history.

Salamanca's history and architecture are a testament to its long and storied past. From its Roman foundations and Moorish influences to its Renaissance splendor and medieval streets, the city is an architectural marvel. Whether exploring the ancient Roman Bridge, wandering through its medieval streets, or visiting its historical landmarks and monuments, Salamanca offers a deep and immersive experience into the cultural and architectural heritage of Spain. Each building, street, and monument holds a story waiting to be discovered, making Salamanca a must-visit destination for history and architecture lovers alike.

Chapter 15: Practical Information for Travelers

Salamanca, a city rich in history, culture, and academic tradition, is an increasingly popular destination for travelers from around the world. With its historic sites, vibrant atmosphere, and welcoming locals, the city offers much to explore. However, to make your visit as smooth and enjoyable as possible, it is essential to be well-prepared. This chapter provides practical information on currency, emergency contacts, local customs, language tips, safety, and public transport to help ensure your time in Salamanca is both comfortable and memorable.

Currency and Local Banking

Spain, including Salamanca, is part of the Eurozone, so the official currency is the Euro (€). The Euro is widely accepted across the city, and many establishments, including shops, restaurants, and hotels, will quote prices in Euros. While credit and debit cards are commonly used, it is always a good idea to carry a small amount of cash for places that do not accept cards, such as small shops or local markets.

Exchanging Currency

If you're traveling from outside the Eurozone, you will need to exchange your currency for Euros. Currency exchange services are available at the airport, major banks, and exchange offices (known as "Oficinas de cambio"). However, be aware of the potential fees and unfavorable exchange rates at airport exchange counters. To get the best exchange rates, it is advisable to use local banks or withdraw cash directly from ATMs.

ATMs are widely available throughout Salamanca, including at the Plaza Mayor and the University of Salamanca, so you can withdraw Euros easily with your credit or debit card. Many ATMs in Spain offer a language option in English, so the process is straightforward for international travelers.

Banking in Salamanca

Banks in Salamanca are generally open from 8:30 AM to 2:00 PM, Monday to Friday, with extended hours on Thursdays in some branches. Most banks are closed on weekends, although some larger international banks may offer weekend services. Bank branches are often located near Plaza Mayor and along major streets like Calle de Toro.

If you need to open a local bank account for an extended stay, it is best to visit a branch directly. Many of the major Spanish banks, such as Banco Santander, BBVA, and Caixabank, have branches in Salamanca.

Emergency Contacts and Medical Services

Traveling to a new city means understanding how to handle potential emergencies. Salamanca is a relatively safe city, but it's always good to be prepared for the unexpected. This section provides key emergency contacts and medical services information for your peace of mind.

Emergency Contacts

Spain has a single emergency number for all types of emergencies: 112. This number can be dialed for ambulance, police, or fire emergencies. The operator will assist you in Spanish, but English-speaking operators are often available in major cities, including Salamanca.

Local police can be reached at 092, while the civil guard can be contacted via 062 in case of more serious law enforcement issues. For less urgent police matters or to file a report, the Policía Nacional can be contacted at 091.

Medical Services

Spain has a highly regarded healthcare system, and Salamanca is home to both public and private medical facilities. If you are visiting from the EU, ensure you carry your European Health Insurance Card (EHIC), which entitles you to receive healthcare on the same terms as Spanish citizens. For non-EU travelers, travel insurance that covers medical expenses is highly recommended.

Salamanca has several public hospitals and clinics, including the Hospital Universitario de Salamanca, located at Calle de Villamayor, which provides emergency and specialized care. The Clínica Universidad de Salamanca is another well-known facility that offers comprehensive medical services.

If you need a pharmacy, they are easy to find throughout the city, marked by a green cross symbol. Many pharmacies in Salamanca offer 24-hour services for emergency medical supplies, over-the-counter medications, and basic health advice.

Local Customs and Etiquette

Understanding local customs and etiquette is an essential part of respecting the culture of any city you visit, and Salamanca is no exception. While the city is welcoming to tourists, being aware of Spanish social norms will help you enjoy a smoother and more respectful stay.

Greetings and Social Etiquette

In Spain, people are generally warm and informal in their greetings, especially in smaller cities like Salamanca. It's customary to greet people with a friendly "Hola" (hello) or "Buenos días" (good morning). Handshakes are common among acquaintances, but in more familiar settings, kissing on both cheeks (starting with the left cheek) is a typical greeting.

When addressing people, especially in formal situations, use the formal "usted" instead of "tú" (the informal "you"), unless you are invited to use the latter. This is particularly important in interactions with older people or those in positions of authority, like in shops or restaurants.

Dining Etiquette

Spanish meals are typically served later than in other countries, and the typical lunch hour is around 2:00 PM to 3:00 PM, while dinner is often not served until 9:00 PM or 10:00 PM. Be prepared for the restaurant atmosphere to be much quieter during earlier hours, with most locals eating later in the evening.

When eating out, you can expect tapas (small appetizers) to be served with drinks, especially in bars. It's common to share these tapas with your companions. At sit-down restaurants, always wait for the host to offer a seat, and be mindful of table manners—keep your hands on the table (not in your lap) and refrain from talking with your mouth full.

Tipping

Tipping in Salamanca is not as compulsory as it is in other countries, but it is always appreciated. In restaurants, it is common to leave a tip of around 5-10% of the total bill if the service was satisfactory. In cafes and bars, rounding up the bill is also acceptable. For taxi drivers, it's customary to round up to the nearest Euro.

Language Tips and Basic Phrases

Spanish is the official language of Salamanca, and while many locals understand and speak basic English, especially in tourist areas, knowing a few key phrases in Spanish will go a long way in helping you navigate the city and interact with locals.

Basic Spanish Phrases for Travelers

Here are some basic phrases that will be helpful during your stay in Salamanca:

- ¡Hola! (Hello!)

- Buenos días (Good morning)

- Buenas tardes (Good afternoon)

- Buenas noches (Good evening)

- ¿Cómo estás? (How are you?)

- Muy bien, gracias. ¿Y tú? (Very well, thank you. And you?)

- ¿Dónde está...? (Where is...?)

- ¿Cuánto cuesta? (How much does it cost?)

- ¿Habla inglés? (Do you speak English?)

- Perdón, ¿puedo ayudarte? (Excuse me, can I help you?)

- ¿Me puede dar la cuenta? (Can you give me the bill?)

- Tengo una reserva (I have a reservation)

Learning a few basic phrases will help you feel more comfortable and build rapport with locals. Don't be discouraged if your Spanish isn't perfect—most Spaniards appreciate the effort to speak their language.

Safety Tips for Travelers

Salamanca is generally considered a safe city for tourists, with low crime rates compared to larger Spanish cities. However, like any destination, it's important to stay alert and take basic precautions to ensure a safe and enjoyable trip.

Pickpocketing and Theft

Pickpocketing can be an issue in busy areas like Plaza Mayor and Calle de Toro, especially in crowded public spaces. Be sure to keep an eye on your personal belongings, especially in crowded tourist attractions and public transport. It's advisable to use a money belt or secure backpack to protect valuables.

Avoiding Scams

While Salamanca is a safe city, tourists should be cautious of potential scams. Be wary of anyone who approaches you offering unsolicited help or trying to sell items aggressively. Always use reputable services for taxis and tours. If you're uncertain about the legitimacy of an offer or deal, it's best to politely decline.

Health and Safety

Salamanca has a strong healthcare system, but it's important to have travel insurance that covers emergency medical expenses, especially for non-EU visitors. Keep a list of emergency contacts, including the nearest hospital and your country's embassy or consulate.

As with any other city, avoid walking alone late at night in poorly lit areas and be cautious when using ATMs after dark. Stick to well-lit streets and always be aware of your surroundings.

How to Use Public Transport in Salamanca

Salamanca has an efficient and convenient public transport system that includes buses and taxis, making it easy for visitors to navigate the city and explore its many attractions. Understanding how to use these services will make your stay more comfortable.

Buses

Salamanca's bus system is operated by Salamanca City Bus, and it covers the city center and surrounding neighborhoods. Buses are a great way to travel between major attractions, parks, and residential areas. Bus stops are clearly marked, and routes are listed in the bus timetables. Tickets are typically purchased from machines at the bus stop or paid directly to the driver when boarding.

A single bus ride costs around 1.30 EUR, but discounted passes are available for those staying in the city for a longer period. Bus tickets can be purchased on-board or at kiosks. The buses are clean, punctual, and a reliable mode of transport for navigating the city.

Taxis

Taxis in Salamanca are easy to find, with taxis available at designated taxi stands or via taxi-hailing apps. The official taxi vehicles are usually white with a yellow stripe on the side, and all taxis are equipped with taximeters to calculate the fare based on distance. The base fare for a taxi ride within the city is approximately 3 EUR, with additional charges for luggage or trips outside the city center.

Taxis are a good option for visitors who need to reach destinations not well-served by buses or for those traveling with large groups or heavy luggage.

Bicycle Rentals

Salamanca has a growing network of bicycle lanes, making it an ideal city for cycling. Several bike rental services are available for tourists, offering an eco-friendly way to explore the city at your own pace. Many public bike rental stations can be found around the city, where you can rent bikes for a few hours or an entire day.

Salamanca is a city that offers a wealth of cultural experiences, historical landmarks, and welcoming locals, and understanding the practical aspects of traveling to this beautiful city can make your trip more enjoyable. From the currency and banking system to safety tips, language basics, and public transport information, this chapter has provided the essential information you need to navigate Salamanca with ease.

Printed in Dunstable, United Kingdom